MAKING

CURRICULUM

MATTER

Also by Angela Di Michele Lalor

Ensuring High-Quality Curriculum: How to Design, Revise, or Adopt Curriculum Aligned to Student Success

ANGELA DI MICHELE LALOR

MAKING

CURRICULUM

MATTER

How to Build SEL, Equity, and
Other Priorities into Daily Instruction

ascd

Alexandria, Virginia USA

1703 N. Beauregard St. • Alexandria, VA 22311-1714 USA
Phone: 800-933-2723 or 703-578-9600 • Fax: 703-575-5400
Website: www.ascd.org • Email: member@ascd.org
Author guidelines: www.ascd.org/write

Ranjit Sidhu, *CEO & Executive Director;* Penny Reinart, *Chief Impact Officer;* Genny Ostertag, *Senior Director, Editing & Acquisitions;* Julie Houtz, *Director, Book Editing;* Liz Wegner, *Editor;* Thomas Lytle, *Creative Director;* Donald Ely, *Art Director;* Melissa Johnston, *Graphic Designer;* Valerie Younkin, *Senior Production Designer;* Kelly Marshall, *Production Manager;* Shajuan Martin, *E-Publishing Specialist;* Christopher Logan, *Senior Production Specialist*

Copyright © 2021 ASCD. All rights reserved. It is illegal to reproduce copies of this work in print or electronic format (including reproductions displayed on a secure intranet or stored in a retrieval system or other electronic storage device from which copies can be made or displayed) without the prior written permission of the publisher. By purchasing only authorized electronic or print editions and not participating in or encouraging piracy of copyrighted materials, you support the rights of authors and publishers. Readers who wish to reproduce or republish excerpts of this work in print or electronic format may do so for a small fee by contacting the Copyright Clearance Center (CCC), 222 Rosewood Dr., Danvers, MA 01923, USA (phone: 978-750-8400; fax: 978-646-8600; web: www.copyright.com). To inquire about site licensing options or any other reuse, contact ASCD Permissions at www.ascd.org/permissions or permissions@ascd.org. For a list of vendors authorized to license ASCD e-books to institutions, see www.ascd.org/epubs. Send translation inquiries to translations@ascd.org.

ASCD® is a registered trademark of Association for Supervision and Curriculum Development. All other trademarks contained in this book are the property of, and reserved by, their respective owners, and are used for editorial and informational purposes only. No such use should be construed to imply sponsorship or endorsement of the book by the respective owners.

All web links in this book are correct as of the publication date below but may have become inactive or otherwise modified since that time. If you notice a deactivated or changed link, please email books@ascd.org with the words "Link Update" in the subject line. In your message, please specify the web link, the book title, and the page number on which the link appears.

PAPERBACK ISBN: 978-1-4166-3023-4   ASCD product #122007 n7/21

PDF E-BOOK ISBN: 978-1-4166-3024-1; see Books in Print for other formats.

Quantity discounts are available: email programteam@ascd.org or call 800-933-2723, ext. 5773, or 703-575-5773. For desk copies, go to www.ascd.org/deskcopy.

Library of Congress Cataloging-in-Publication Data
Names: Lalor, Angela Di Michele, author.
Title: Making curriculum matter : how to build SEL, equity, and other priorities into daily instruction / Angela Di Michele Lalor.
Description: Alexandria : ASCD, 2021. | Includes bibliographical references and index.
Identifiers: LCCN 2021011319 (print) | LCCN 2021011320 (ebook) | ISBN 9781416630234 (paperback) | ISBN 9781416630241 (pdf)
Subjects: LCSH: Education—Curricula. | Educational equalization. | Affective education. | Service learning.
Classification: LCC LB1570 .L35 2021 (print) | LCC LB1570 (ebook) | DDC 375—dc23
LC record available at https://lccn.loc.gov/2021011319
LC ebook record available at https://lccn.loc.gov/2021011320

To my family, who anchor me and inspire me,
especially Bill, William, Catherine,
Joseph, Mom, and Dad

MAKING

CURRICULUM

MATTER

How to Build SEL, Equity, and Other Priorities into Daily Instruction

Introduction

The word cloud shown in Figure I.1 represents what can happen in the minds of teachers, administrators, and other school personnel when they think about what to teach and how. Each area of focus makes sense individually; for example, educators would readily agree that schools are responsible for the intellectual, social, and emotional learning of their students. However, when thought of collectively, these same areas of focus can feel overwhelming, as jumbled as the word cloud, often making educators feel pulled in many directions.

Figure I.1

EDUCATOR'S WORD CLOUD

In this book, I introduce five elements of a curriculum that matters—*practices, deep thinking, social and emotional learning, civic engagement and discourse,* and *equity*—as a way of unjumbling the cloud (see Figure I.2). By doing so, I present a framework for examining how these key areas fit into curriculum and instruction and interact to produce cohesive, meaningful learning. The elements attach specific language to what matters in schools. They are categorical in nature because they label important outcomes for learning yet provide each school the necessary leeway for having its own approach, enabling curriculum and instruction to be responsive to the students and community that the school serves.

Figure I.2
THE FIVE ELEMENTS OF A CURRICULUM THAT MATTERS

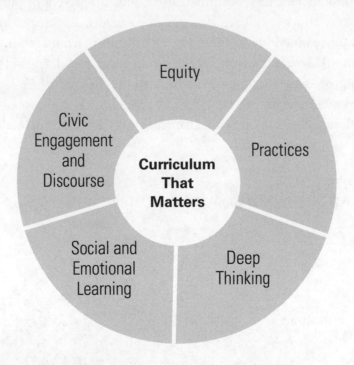

In the first chapter, I describe how schools communicate what matters through their words and actions and the relationship between valued outcomes and the curriculum. I connect those values to the framework of a curriculum that matters and present a tool for you to use, in the form of chapter reflections, as you think about your curriculum and classroom practices. Using this tool while reading the remaining chapters will guide you on the best entry point for creating your own curriculum that matters.

The next five chapters of the book examine the elements individually. Each chapter presents a rationale behind the importance of the element, ways to incorporate the element into the curriculum, and strategies for immediately addressing the element in classroom instruction. This structure provides a way for you to examine how the elements exist in your curriculum while considering immediate actions for modification and implementation.

As you read through the description of each element, you should begin to see how they overlap, as shown in Figure I.3. The overlap is natural and necessary. Designing a curriculum that matters is about changing the lens for viewing, discussing, and implementing the curriculum and not necessarily about adding more to what happens in the classroom. A deep understanding of each element is essential for effectively integrating them into the curriculum and implementing them in the classroom in a way that will have a positive effect on student learning.

Figure I.3

OVERLAPPING ELEMENTS IN A CURRICULUM THAT MATTERS

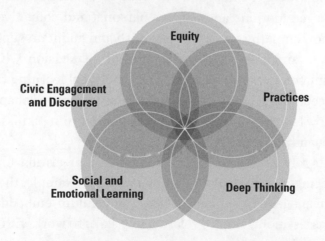

The first element, examined in Chapter 2, is *practices*. A practice is generally defined as a customary or habitual way of doing something. Practices are used by historians, mathematicians, scientists, artists, musicians, and other specialists in their field. For example, a historian contextualizes primary-source documents by noting who wrote the document, when it was written, and the events occurring in the world at that time. As historians repeatedly draw upon the skills involved in contextualization, the skill is considered a practice. A practice may consist of one or more skills but could also include a way of thinking, a procedure, or an approach. Practices are used to make sense of discipline-specific information, and they allow students to work with content in authentic ways.

Chapter 3 explores the element of *deep thinking*. Deep thinking involves moving from a general understanding of content, knowledge, and ideas to thinking that allows for application, extension, and creation of new ideas. We look at how students apply deep thinking to multistep, complex tasks that require the use of different levels of cognition and knowledge (Anderson & Krathwohl, 2001). We examine design thinking and creative thinking and consider their related instructional practices as illustrations of deep thinking at work in the classroom.

In Chapter 4, the focus turns to the element of *social and emotional learning*. According to the Collaborative for Academic, Social, and Emotional Learning (CASEL), social and emotional learning (SEL) is "the process through which all young people and adults acquire and apply the knowledge, skills, and attitudes to develop healthy identities, manage emotions and achieve personal and collective goals, feel and show empathy for others, establish and maintain supportive relationships, and make responsible and caring decisions" (CASEL, 2020). Many schools address social and emotional learning through programs separate from the general curriculum. In this chapter, we examine how to integrate social and emotional learning skills into the curriculum and daily instruction.

Students rely heavily on social and emotional learning strategies when engaging in a curriculum that matters. For example, they draw upon self-management skills to navigate curriculum-embedded performance assessment, employ relationship skills to work with others, and engage in self-reflection when setting and monitoring goals. These opportunities allow students to practice the skills necessary to become self-regulated, independent learners. This chapter also explores how to address students' mindset so they use SEL skills to foster learning and develop the forbearance necessary to overcome obstacles that may emerge along the way.

Chapter 5 examines curriculum through the lens of *civic engagement and discourse*. A curriculum that matters creates opportunities for students to engage in all levels of community, whether local, state, national, or global. Students learn civic engagement by selecting problems of concern, investigating solutions, and developing actionable plans to address them. The natural audience and beneficiary of student work becomes the community itself.

Effective civic participation requires skill in civic discourse. A curriculum that promotes civic engagement and discourse provides students with strategies and protocols that enhance communication. Students engage in discussions that challenge their thinking and help them to understand experiences, beliefs, opinions, and perspectives other than their own. This chapter also examines the effective use of media-literacy skills so students can select, evaluate, and use information to ground their discourse and actions.

The sequence of chapters about the individual elements of a curriculum that matters begins with *practices* and ends with an examination of *equity*. The order illustrates how each element builds upon and connects to the next, with the ultimate goal of providing an excellent and equitable education for all students. Chapter 6 explains how actions shared in the previous chapters provide the foundation for an equitable education. However, only through the hard work of carefully examining their personal identity can educators design and implement a curriculum that does not unintentionally carry their biases into the curriculum.

Chapter 7 invites you to reflect on what you have learned about the elements and how they fit into your own practice as you consider the entry point best suited to your work in creating a curriculum that matters. Each school will have a different starting point. For schools just beginning their journey, examining practices may be the most logical first step. Teachers who identify themselves as content specialists or have a more traditional view of schools as solely academic institutions will be most ready to make this shift. This observation, however, does not mean that the element of *practices* is the starting point for everyone. The reflection charts at the end of each chapter will help you to recognize what you do well and what elements need further investigation. They will provide insight into where to begin so all students engage in equitable learning experiences.

It is important that I acknowledge that although this book was conceptualized long ago, I wrote and rewrote most of it during the COVID-19 pandemic. As you read through the chapters, you will see examples related to learning during this time.

As I finish this book during the summer of 2020, with schools facing a great deal of uncertainty about what lies ahead, I believe that the framework for a curriculum that matters is more necessary than ever. One lesson learned from the past year is the importance of technology to learning. Technology, however, is not a separate element but rather a tool for engaging with each element. Students use technology as a *practice*. Technology provides tools for engaging in tasks that promote *deep thinking*. Students apply *social and emotional* competencies to engage with others and monitor their learning in both synchronous and asynchronous learning environments. Students can *engage in their community* to support others using online structures.

The need for technology during the pandemic revealed the inequities that exist in education and creates a call to action. Nevertheless, because of educators' resiliency, schools found ways during the pandemic to connect with their students so they could learn. Moving forward, students should never be in this position again.

The ideas I share throughout the book are reminders of what should be regardless of circumstance. I am asking schools to break from the traditional and experiment with the unknown, and to demonstrate the mindset necessary to do so. Now, more than ever, these elements of a curriculum that matters, with their foundation in the vision and mission of schools, are essential. It is my hope that the framework and strategies presented in this book can help educators create schools where students

- Pursue their own pathway in life that is built off students' interests and talents.

- Think deeply and develop a critical consciousness of the world around them.
- Work with and develop strong relationships with others.
- Participate as active members of their communities.
- Are independent and self-regulated learners.
- Develop a deeper understanding of their own and others' identities.
- Are healthy and happy individuals.

What Matters
to Your School?

In most schools, students, parents, and visitors are welcomed with banners and signs that display clear statements of vision and mission, such as these:

> We believe that students should learn in a safe, supportive, and student-centered environment. We are committed to meeting the needs of all students, helping them to achieve academic excellence, and preparing them for a global society.

> We will provide our students with a safe, supportive environment and prepare them with the knowledge, values, and skills to become responsible citizens in a diverse global society.

> We will work together with our community to provide an equitable education where all students can develop personally and academically.

Although their wording may differ slightly, the statements focus on students' academic and social well-being with the intent of preparing them for the world beyond the classroom. The vision statement and its accompanying mission statement serve as the first form of communicating what matters in a school. They, along with other evidence that can be observed and collected through both informal and formal methods, can help schools define what matters and serve as the basis for decision making, including what curriculum and instructional practices teachers use in their classrooms.

This chapter examines how schools communicate what matters through their words and actions, and it considers how the curriculum, used by teachers to make decisions every day, should reflect these valued outcomes. The process of aligning curriculum to what is valued begins by establishing personalized criteria for its design. Although the criteria will reflect the school's unique community, the curriculum should not be limited by what is known and familiar. Every curriculum should address the elements of the framework presented in this book, with its intended goal of providing all students with an excellent and equitable education. The chapter ends with a tool that enables you to make connections between the framework and your school's curriculum and classroom practices.

Three Questions for Schools

To identify what they value for their students, schools should answer three questions: *What does our school say about what it values? How does our school show what it values? How does our curriculum demonstrate what is valued?* Let's take a closer look at each of these.

What Does Our School Say About What It Values?

When carefully considered and thoughtfully prepared, vision and mission statements can be essential to communicating what matters and guiding district and school policies and practices. The vision statement articulates the desired outcome, and the mission statement provides direction for how to achieve this goal. Yvette Jackson (2016) writes of how acknowledging the power of language in vision and mission statements is the first step in ensuring equity for all students:

> When districts embrace belief in and the value of the innate potential of all their students, these beliefs and values are clearly articulated in their vision and mission statements. Mediators astutely recognize the power of language to broadcast a message of equity and excellence. (p. 85)

Given their potential power, the words of the vision and mission statements should not be taken lightly. If written and used as intended, the statements serve as the basis for decision making and as the catalyst for developing a school that lives what it believes. A discussion of the vision and mission statements is an obvious place to start in identifying what matters to your school or classroom. For some, a return to the vision and mission statements may remind them of the school's intention. A review of the statements may also lead to revisions. Some teachers might even be inspired to write student-friendly statements for their own classrooms, which become even more powerful if students are involved in creating them.

How Does Our School Show What It Values?

Evidence of what matters abounds in schools—in what hangs in the hallway, what happens in the classroom, what is scheduled on the calendar, and what is written in communications. For example, consider the following description of an elementary school: Hallways are lined with student writings that represent a wide range of content, genres, and authentic experiences. The 1st grade classrooms display how-to booklets about a process selected by students to showcase their expertise. Outside the 4th grade classrooms are "newspaper accounts" of events that students have participated in within the local community. A peek inside a classroom reveals students working with partners in a peer-review process. One student is intently listening to another's feedback, knowing that his classmate is offering valuable advice that will help him to revise and improve his work. On Mondays after school, teachers meet in the "Zen room" to learn about and practice mindfulness strategies. Teachers share these strategies with their students and integrate them into their daily classroom routines.

School practices such as these reveal what the school values for its students. It is evident that this school values collaboration, reflection, process, application, and mindfulness as outcomes for student learning. However, schools are complex institutions. In this same school, prep books appear the month before the state test, and the school district relies on numerical grades for report cards, indicating an emphasis on traditional forms of assessments and the value placed on state test scores. There may be many reasons for this obvious conflict, as well as a plan in place for addressing the disconnect. What is most important is acknowledging what exists so the school can move forward in providing students with an educational experience aligned to its values and move away from what holds it back.

How Does Our Curriculum Demonstrate What Is Valued?

This book is grounded in the belief that the curriculum is a tool that teachers use to make informed decisions about classroom instruction, so reviewing the current curriculum is an important part of the process. The depth of the analysis can range from a simple read-through, with a listing of what people notice or wonder about, to a formal evaluation.

You may discover that when you decide to examine the curriculum, there is no formal written document or no standard curriculum for teachers at the same grade level or for those teaching the same course. Your search may also reveal that a textbook or a program is considered "the curriculum." These are important findings. The first indicates that not all students are being held to the same expectations, and the second indicates that teachers may not feel they have the flexibility to achieve the goals set forth in the vision and mission statements.

You may also find a traditional curriculum that focuses on content and includes a long list of detailed facts and other information that students "need to know." Often this kind of curriculum results in classrooms where the teacher is at center stage, delivering information in an attempt to "cover" all that needs to be taught by the end of the year.

When a written curriculum is focused on developing conceptual understandings, uses assessments to produce as well as measure learning, and incorporates active learning strategies, it provides a strong foundation for addressing the elements of a curriculum that matters (Lalor, 2017). Reviewing the curriculum provides insight into the gap between the curriculum and the values that have been communicated through the vision and mission statements and school practices.

Determining What Matters in Your School's Curriculum

In the Southampton School District in New York, Superintendent Nicholas J. Dyno was committed to engaging the district in a comprehensive, multiyear curriculum-design initiative that had been carefully laid out with the assistance of Larrilee Jemiola, director of the Peconic Teacher Center, which provides training and resources for teachers. Teachers on special assignment—Kathryn Schreck, Virginia McGovern, Kimberly Milton, John Wendt, and Sean Zay—served as curriculum liaisons, facilitating the design process with teams of teachers.

In the initial stages of the project, the curriculum liaisons worked with district administrators to examine the district's vision and mission statements as well as evidence of the ways in which the district communicated what it valued. District administrators included Julieanne Purcell, executive director of instructional technology; Nancy Wicker, coordinator of instructional practices and staff development; and principals Jaime Bottcher, Tim Frazier, and Brian Zahn. Their examination resulted in the development of the following criteria to guide the design of the Southampton curriculum:

A quality curriculum that educates students in a safe, supportive environment and equips them with the knowledge, values, and skills to become responsible citizens in a dynamic global society—

- Is accessible to staff, students, community.
- Aligns to content and process standards.
- Provides all students with the opportunity to meet standards.
- Includes different assessment types and moments.
- Actively engages students in their learning.
- Represents all stakeholders.
- Incorporates an interdisciplinary approach.
- Addresses dispositions.
- Allows students to engage in service to their community and/or each other.

The criteria provided a way for Southampton to hold the curriculum accountable to the district's values. It would not be possible for Southampton to address all the criteria from the start, but knowing what the expectations were for the curriculum provided a road map for how to achieve them.

Connecting to the Elements of a Curriculum That Matters

The creation of criteria to guide curriculum requires thoughtful reflection about what schools want for their students. As explained in the Introduction, the framework presented in this book provides a way to recognize the necessary elements that build an equitable curriculum. To maximize their impact, the elements need to be examined individually and then collectively for successful implementation in the classroom. Although the elements themselves are not optional, schools do have options about how to approach them. This flexibility is how schools personalize curriculum to their community. If you examine Southampton's criteria in terms of the elements of a curriculum that matters, as shown in Figure 1.1, you will see how they align to the elements.

Not all schools will have the same starting point or design approach. Southampton began with criteria for their curriculum, which led them to an examination of the elements during the design process. When teachers participated in professional development, they simultaneously examined the elements and applied their learning to the design of the curriculum. The criteria for design of the curriculum also evolved and changed as the district engaged in this process.

To help you determine the best approach for entering this process, I suggest using the chart on page 16 to record your thinking as you read through this book.

Guiding questions at the end of Chapters 2 through 6 can help you think about how your school currently addresses the elements, a good potential starting point for your effort, and what areas need the most development. What you do well currently will provide the anchor for the system. This area of strength can be sustained as you work to improve areas that you have not addressed or that need improvement.

Figure 1.1

EXAMPLE OF ALIGNMENT BETWEEN CURRICULUM ELEMENTS AND DISTRICT CURRICULUM CRITERIA

Elements of a Curriculum That Matters	Criteria/Evidence from Southampton School District
Practices: The applications of an idea, a belief, or a method to construct understanding; often associated with specific disciplines but frequently found to be applicable across disciplines.	• Aligns to content and process standards.
Deep Thinking: Thinking that allows for application, extension, and creation of new ideas rather than a general understanding of content, knowledge, and ideas.	• Incorporates an interdisciplinary approach.
Social and Emotional Learning: Learning that includes developing an understanding of one's self to achieve personal goals, understand and appreciate others, self-regulate, develop relationships, and make good decisions.	• Actively engages students in their learning. • Addresses dispositions.
Civic Engagement: Active participation as a local, state, national, or global community member. **Civic Discourse:** Successful participation in conversations with those who do not hold the same view or opinion and to learn from the experience.	• Allows students to engage in service to their community or each other.
Equity: Addressing the individualized attributes of students (e.g., culture, race, gender, ability, language) so they can engage in their learning, and eliminating those practices that prevent students from reaching their full potential.	• Is accessible to staff, students, community. • Provides all students with the opportunity to meet standards. • Represents all stakeholders. • Includes different assessment types and moments.

REFLECTION CHART FOR ELEMENTS OF A CURRICULUM THAT MATTERS

Practices: The applications of an idea, a belief, or a method to construct understanding; often associated with specific disciplines but frequently found to be applicable across disciplines.

Strengths, Needs, and Possible Next Steps

Deep Thinking: Thinking that allows for application, extension, and creation of new ideas rather than a general understanding of content, knowledge, and ideas.

Strengths, Needs, and Possible Next Steps

Social and Emotional Learning: Learning that includes developing an understanding of one's self to achieve personal goals, understand and appreciate others, self-regulate, develop relationships, and make good decisions.

Strengths, Needs, and Possible Next Steps

Civic Engagement: Active participation as a local, state, national, or global community member. **Civic Discourse:** Successful participation in conversations with those who do not hold the same view or opinion and to learn from the experience.

Strengths, Needs, and Possible Next Steps

Equity: Addressing the individualized attributes of students (e.g., culture, race, gender, ability, language) so they can engage in their learning, and eliminating those practices that prevent students from reaching their full potential.

Strengths, Needs, and Possible Next Steps

The goal of this book is not to create "more" for a school to incorporate into the curriculum and for teachers to implement in the classroom. The process would be overwhelming if every element became a priority, competing for attention and fidelity in implementation and taxing an already strained system. In that case, the result could be surface-level implementation with little to no impact—the opposite of the intended outcome.

The goal of this book is to help schools see what exists more clearly and through different lenses and to ensure all students have the opportunity to learn from a curriculum that matters. The next five chapters provide an in-depth look at each element to support its strategic integration into the curriculum and seamless implementation into classroom instruction.

Summing Up

Schools can identify what they value for their students by answering three important questions: *What does our school say about what it values? How does our school show what it values? How does our curriculum demonstrate what is valued?* The reflection prompted by these questions provides schools with insight into the degree to which their curriculum aligns with what they value. The entry point into the design of a curriculum that matters will vary by school. Examining how your school addresses each element will help you decide on the best starting point for incorporating the elements of a curriculum that matters to ensure an excellent and equitable education for all students.

Practices

Consider the following scenarios:

> A group of cryptographers is working to come up with a more effective way to prevent malicious attacks on sensitive data. If successful, their new encryption technique will make it safer for financial institutions to conduct transactions for their customers and prevent hackers from gaining access to important information such as birth dates, social security numbers, and account numbers.

> A chemical engineer works in his lab to use the technique of emulsion to improve the quality of a sunscreen product. Reducing the thickness of the cream may convince more people to use the product daily to protect their skin from the harmful effects of the sun.

> A docent at the local historical museum is preparing a new tour for the community's elementary students. She is highlighting key artifacts in a typical 19th-century farmhouse that will help students compare life in the past with life today.

Each example involves people who are relying on practices that are fundamental to their field of work. The cryptographers decontextualize the mathematical problem and represent it symbolically; they persevere through multiple attempts to solve it to improve the software. The chemical engineer plans and conducts an investigation, analyzing and interpreting the data to increase the effectiveness and consistency of the sunscreen product. The docent gathers, uses, and interprets historical evidence to make decisions about tour stops and artifact displays so the students leave with an understanding of the concepts of continuity and change. *Practices* allow these professionals to apply their content expertise in practical and beneficial ways that are integral to the work that they do.

These real-life examples illustrate the importance of looking beyond just the content of a unit of study to the approaches for working with that content in a meaningful way. A curriculum that matters ensures the strategic use of practices to support learning.

Practices are the customary, habitual, or expected procedures or ways of applying an idea, a belief, or a method to construct understanding. They are often associated with specific disciplines but are frequently applicable across disciplines. Although a practice may consist of one or more skills, it goes beyond skill because it is used in the context of understanding and not focused on the duplication of steps isolated from a greater purpose.

When we think of practices in a real-world context, it is easy to recognize the need to address them in the classroom. Content knowledge remains fundamental to working with practices, but it should not be the sole purpose of learning in schools. In today's interconnected world, with easy access to large quantities of information, schools need to move from transmitting information to focusing on what to do with that information—in other words, schools need to focus on practices.

National and state educational organizations have recognized this reality and have communicated the need to move beyond the "what" to the important understandings, skills, and processes that are essential to the specific disciplines they represent. For example, the Next Generation Science Standards (NGSS) created a framework focused on three dimensions:

1. *Practices* expand on what is meant by inquiry in science by describing the work of scientists and engineers so that students can engage in similar experiences.

2. *Cross-Cutting Concepts* focus on concepts that allow students to make connections across four major science domains: physical sciences; life sciences; earth and space sciences; and engineering, technology, and applications of science.
3. *Disciplinary Core Ideas* identify content understandings and scaffold learning in the four major science domains across grade levels. (National Research Council, 2013)

These three dimensions are the basis of the science performance expectations that help students build foundational knowledge of how science is applied in the real world.

The Science and Engineering Practices focus specifically on cognitive, social, and physical actions students use as scientists investigating the world around them and as engineers designing and building models and other representations to solve problems (National Research Council, 2013). For example, consider a task in which high school students are asked to evaluate a medical treatment and explain the benefits and disadvantages of using nuclear radiation in treating patients. Students use several science and engineering practices to complete the task. They *develop a model* to illustrate how energy is released and the relationships between components underlying the nuclear processes. Students then *use their model and additional research as evidence* in their evaluation of the medical treatment.

The Next Generation Science Standards are not the only organizational standards that recognize the importance of practices. Other national affiliations, as well as state and local education boards, have articulated important practices that are integral to the discipline. The Standards for Mathematical Practices (CCSS, 2019), the Historical Thinking Skills (College Board, 2012), and the Creative Practices for the Arts (NCCAS, 2014) are just a few of the many examples available to educators as they begin to think about viewing their curriculum through the lens of practices and shifting instruction to emphasize their importance.

Curriculum Through the Lens of Practices

Of all the elements of a curriculum that matters, *practices* is the one most directly linked to content. It is the element that is most within reach for a school transitioning from a traditional model of schooling to one that encompasses valued outcomes.

A curriculum that matters ensures strong alignment to the practices associated with a specific discipline, as well as to content standards. Strong alignment is evident when the student task and the learning expectation are so interwoven it is difficult to separate the two (Lalor, 2017). For example, at the high school level, the New York State Social Studies practice of "Chronological Reasoning and Causation" calls for students to "articulate how events are related to one another in time and explain the ways in which earlier ideas and events may influence subsequent ideas and events" (NYSED, 2017c). A task that is weakly aligned to practices would simply ask students to answer questions about a timeline that shows events leading to and following the U.S. Civil War. The task is weakly aligned because it focuses solely on events, and not necessarily ideas, and is confined to one time period. In a strongly aligned task, students would analyze a variety of primary and secondary sources to create an annotated timeline that shows the progression of ideas and events, beginning with the Civil War and leading to the civil rights movement of the 1960s and today. In this task, students are examining both events and ideas and connecting them across time.

Strong alignment begins with explicitly identifying the practices that will be taught and assessed in each unit of study. "Taught and assessed" means that the practice will be identified for the student and that the student will learn specific strategies for using the practice. Students' use of the practice is monitored through formative assessment and evaluated with a summative assessment. Practices that are taught and assessed are different from those that are "addressed." When a practice is addressed, it is touched upon or revisited from a previous unit. It is not central to the learning in the unit. This distinction helps teachers know what to emphasize in instruction.

In addition to explicitly identifying the practices that are taught and assessed in the unit, a curriculum that values practices will explain how the practice is used by the student in the unit. For example, let's examine the Common Core State Standards for Mathematical Practices:

1. Make sense of problems and persevere in solving them.
2. Reason abstractly and quantitatively.
3. Construct viable arguments and critique the reasoning of others.
4. Model with mathematics.
5. Use appropriate tools strategically.
6. Attend to precision.
7. Look for and make use of structure.
8. Look for and express regularity in repeated reasoning. (CCSS, 2019)

In reviewing these practices, a common reaction might be that they all apply to every unit. Although there is some truth to this reaction, students will not be able to use the practices fluidly unless they are given direct instruction and opportunities to practice each one in relation to specific concepts.

To make them practical for teachers to use and to convey their importance to students, each practice needs to be unpacked in the curriculum document to explain its connection to the concepts taught within the unit. For example, the practice "model with mathematics" can include the use of diagrams, charts, graphs, flowcharts, and formulas. Kindergartners use modeling with mathematics when they deconstruct objects as math drawings and addition equations. Sixth graders apply the practice when they use vertical and horizontal number lines to visualize integers and to understand their connection to whole numbers. And finally, it is reinforced in algebra, when students construct and interpret two-way tables and scatter-plots to summarize and graph bivariate numerical data and use linear, exponential, and quadratic models to describe numerical relationships. The application changes, but in each case, students develop the understanding that models can be used to visualize and understand mathematics. To improve the likelihood that teachers will integrate that practice into their instruction, the curriculum document must clearly explain the practice and its specific application within the unit.

Like the learning activities, the assessment plan should demonstrate explicit alignment to practices. Traditionally, assessment blueprints used to ensure the validity of tests have consisted of a simple listing of the question number, the answer and rationale, and the corresponding standard. In a quality curriculum, the primary means of assessment is a curriculum-embedded performance assessment that *produces* as well as measures learning. It requires that students pursue deep conceptual understanding and apply their learning for an authentic purpose or audience (Lalor, 2017). Curriculum-embedded performance assessments naturally allow students to apply practices as would professionals in the field.

To ensure the validity of such assessments, they too require an assessment blueprint. Figure 2.1 shows a transdisciplinary curriculum-embedded performance assessment created by a team of teachers in Connecticut's Norwalk School District as part of a districtwide STEAM initiative led by Chief Academic Officer Brenda Myers. Headed by Tina Henckel, K–12 director of STEM; Jennifer Katona, visual and performing arts senior manager; and Kate Curran, STEM teacher in residence, the team included teachers Mary Anderson, Margaret Ferrari, Avery Gomez, Isaac Iwuagwu, Patrick Jeanetti, Kathleen Meehan, Fred Pierre-Louis, Jacqueline Prinz, and Virginia Seeley; and coaches Daniel Kreiness and Tim Luchsinger. Together they designed a unit of study that would serve as a model for additional curriculum for the new STEAM program at the Ponus Ridge Middle School, under the leadership of Principal Damon Lewis and Assistant Principal Evan Byron.

As part of a transdisciplinary STEAM unit, this curriculum-embedded performance assessment aligns to content standards from multiple disciplines, but the practices are at the core of the experience. Students are working as architects, considering the criteria and constraints of their client and pulling from their knowledge of scientific principles to design an eco-friendly, usable space for their school community. Students model with mathematics and attend to precision as they use precise measurements, labels, and scale to create a blueprint. They use literacy and visual arts practices to effectively

Figure 2.1

PERFORMANCE ASSESSMENT FOR A TRANSDISCIPLINARY STEAM UNIT

Assessment Description	Standards Alignment
Ponus Ridge is opening a new PreK–8 STEAM academy. Currently, there is a courtyard outside the library that is an unused outdoor space. As 8th grade students, you have been chosen to leave the school community a legacy of a multipurpose shared space for future students to enjoy for years to come. You are part of a team that will plan and construct a design for the courtyard that could be used for learning, community building, and social-emotional well-being by the Ponus community. In creating your design, you will need to think about	
• Purpose: for example, how students could use the space together, how teachers could use it with their students, how mentors could use it with their mentees. • Scientific principles such as climate and weathering and their impact on the natural and man-made items within the space. • Impact on the natural environment. • Accessibility to students with differing abilities • Cost of the materials.	**MS-ETS1-1:** Define the criteria and constraints of a design problem.
Your team will create a proposal that includes a blueprint and a written explanation of your plan. The blueprint will include precise measurements and geometrical figures to represent both the natural and man-made elements. The proposal should include the rationale behind your blueprint and an explanation of • How the space should be used, who will use it, and why you are making this recommendation. • The scientific principles that support your selected design and an explanation of the impact of the design on the natural environment. • A budget for the cost of materials and the value to the school and local community in making such an investment.	**CCSS MATH CONTENT 8.G.A.4:** Understand two-dimensional figures. **CCSS MATH PRACTICE 4:** Model with mathematics. **CCSS MATH PRACTICE 6:** Attend to precision. **CCSS.ELA-LITERACY.W.8.2:** Write informative/explanatory texts to examine a topic and convey ideas, concepts, and information through the selection, organization, and analysis of relevant content. **Social Studies ECO 8.1:** Explain how economic decisions affect the well-being of individuals, businesses, and society.

Assessment Description	Standards Alignment
Your proposal will be presented to the administration and construction company for advice on any needed revisions. Your team can edit your proposal based on this advice. Your final idea will be presented to the Princeton 8th graders. In your presentations, you will • Select, organize, and design images and words to make your presentation visually clear and compelling. • Present your proposal, emphasizing salient points in a focused, coherent manner using relevant evidence, sound valid reasoning, and well-chosen details. • Use appropriate eye contact, adequate volume, and clear pronunciation. The 8th graders will then vote on the winning design.	**Visual Arts: Cr2.3.8a:** Select, organize, and design images and words to make visually clear and compelling presentations. **CCSS ELA-LITERACY.SL.8.4:** Present claims and findings, emphasizing salient points in a focused, coherent manner with relevant evidence, sound valid reasoning, and well-chosen details; use appropriate eye contact, adequate volume, and clear pronunciation.

communicate their ideas through their presentation. The emphasis on practices is also apparent in the checklist (Figure 2.2) used to evaluate the resulting student work.

The assessment plan and corresponding checklist illustrate strong alignment among the standards, the student work product, and the criteria for evaluation. Together they create a valid and reliable assessment of student learning that communicates the value of practices.

It is easy to recognize when a curriculum has not been deliberately aligned to practices. Indicators include the following:

• A listing of all practices for each individual unit of study
• A mismatch between the practices listed and those that are taught and assessed
• An omission of practices from the assessment plan
• A relegation of practices to the introduction or a separate section of the curriculum
• No identification of practices

If any of these describe your curriculum's approach to the practice, you will need to employ the alignment strategies described earlier.

Figure 2.2

EVALUATION CHECKLIST FOR STEAM EXAMPLE

Blueprint	The blueprint is a professional, realistic, and accurate plan for the development of the proposed space. It • Reflects the identified purpose of the design. • Considers scientific principles in the placement of natural features and additional structures. • Maximizes the use of the natural environment and materials. • Addresses the needs of differently abled students. • Uses appropriate geometric figures as models of plants and structures. • Precisely scales objects. • Includes precise measurements and labels. • Uses technology (accurate, clear manipulation of the software) to create the blueprint. • Uses a key to convey symbols and important information.
Proposal	The proposal clearly explains the information contained in the blueprint, including • How the space will be used, who will use it, and the benefits of the proposed use. • The scientific principles that support the design and an explanation of the impact of the design on the natural environment. • A budget for the cost of materials and the value to the school and local community in making such an investment. • Appropriate evidence from the blueprint to support the explanation. The written proposal • Uses an organizational structure that is easy to understand and follow. • Includes appropriate charts and/or graphs to support explanations.
Presentation	The presentation of the plan • Selects, organizes, and designs images and words to make the presentation visually clear and compelling. • Emphasizes salient points in a focused, coherent manner. • Uses relevant evidence, sound valid reasoning, and well-chosen details. The presenters use appropriate eye contact, adequate volume, and clear pronunciation when sharing the plan.

Incorporating Practices into Classroom Instruction

Teachers can begin by considering the role of individual student practices in the construction of their lessons and student learning activities. In *Visible Learning for Teachers: Maximizing Impact on Learning,* John Hattie (2012) writes of the importance and impact of the following student-*driven* questions in learning:

- Where am I going? What are my goals?
- How am I going? What progress is being made toward this goal?
- Where to next? What steps need to be made to make better progress?

These questions provide guidance on how to best incorporate practices into classroom lessons. If students are to answer these questions to guide their learning, teachers must plan lessons that make it possible for them to do so.

The first and most important step is identifying a learning target for the lesson. Providing a learning target gives students the information they need to answer the *Where am I going?* question, which is the precursor to the remaining questions. When the learning target focuses on a practice, students have information that helps them to understand how they can use a practice to learn and apply content.

A learning target communicates what students need to know and be able to do. Targets are usually written as "I can" or "We will" statements and shared at the beginning of class.

Let's examine a learning target written by Suzana Blanco, a 10th grade teacher in the Southampton School District in New York. Suzana shared this target with her students during a lesson I observed in her classroom: "I can determine how the agricultural revolution impacted Great Britain by examining how the country changed over time." This learning target communicated the following social studies practice: "Students will distinguish between long-term and immediate causes and multiple effects to understand change."

The practice was clearly evident in what the students were doing in the classroom. Students worked in small groups to analyze primary sources. For each primary source, they needed to determine if the author had presented a change resulting from the agricultural revolution, whether the change was immediate or occurred after the time period of the agricultural revolution, and what kind of change was described—political, economic, or social. After examining the documents, each group shared what they learned and how the documents supported their conclusions.

To further help students monitor their progress and adjust strategies, teachers can also include success criteria as part of the learning target. Success criteria expand on what students can do to reach the learning target. For example, adding success criteria to Suzana's learning target elaborates on what students do when examining change over time:

> I can determine the impact of the agricultural revolution in Great Britain by
>
> • Identifying immediate social, political, and economic changes.
> • Making connections between immediate and long-term changes.

For this learning target, the success criteria provide additional information for students—namely, that change can affect social, political, and economic aspects of a nation and that examining change means looking at both immediate and long-term change. While the students in Suzana's class engage in these actions, the success criteria put language to the steps they are using to complete the task. This information helps students further understand not only the agricultural revolution in Great Britain but any event resulting in change.

This type of learning target paired with success criteria is much different from some of the learning targets I have seen in classrooms, many of which focus on what students will do. A learning target that reads "I can examine the agricultural revolution in Great Britain by completing a timeline" identifies the task the students will complete (what they are doing) but not what they should be thinking about in the process. Focusing on the thinking develops the transferable skill necessary for using a practice to learn. The chart in Figure 2.3 illustrates how a learning target can evolve from a statement of content and task to include a practice and provide success criteria.

Figure 2.3

TYPES OF LEARNING TARGETS

Learning Target Focused on Content and Task	Learning Target That Includes a Practice	Learning Target That Includes a Practice and Success Criteria
I can examine the agricultural revolution in Great Britain by completing a timeline.	I can determine how the agricultural revolution affected Great Britain by examining how the country changed over time.	I can determine the impact of the agricultural revolution in Great Britain by • Identifying immediate social, political, and economic changes. • Making connections between immediate and long-term changes.

The posting and sharing of learning targets and success criteria are the first steps in addressing John Hattie's questions. In addition to engaging in learning activities that strongly align to practice, students should be able to reference the learning target and success criteria during the lesson to monitor their understanding. It is important here to notice that the focus is on what students do. Practices, like all standards, are written in terms of *student* actions and not *teacher* actions. In designing lessons that align to practices, teachers must consider how the student will use the practice during the lesson. It is not enough for a teacher to model a practice in use or to talk about how it can be used. Students must engage with the practice itself.

For example, the artistic processes shared by all arts disciplines include creating, performing/producing/presenting, responding, and connecting. Responding is the act of understanding and evaluating how the arts convey meaning. It involves understanding how perception influences the analysis of art and interpreting the intent and meaning of artistic work (NCCAS, 2014). A teacher who shares and critiques the work of Diego Rivera has not engaged students with the practice. For students to engage, they must conduct research on Rivera, determine how his life influenced his work, and use their own perception to analyze a piece on their own or with peers. This is not to say that the teacher sharing her perception or analysis has no value;

but for the practice to become a tool for learning, students must have multiple opportunities to use it themselves.

To help students use the practice, the learning target and success criteria must also be visible and referenced throughout the lesson, giving students the opportunity to answer the questions *How am I doing?* and *Where to next?* Many elementary teachers have already developed this routine by displaying anchor charts in the classroom. These valuable charts identify important steps in a process, similar to the thinking outlined in success criteria for achieving the learning target. For example, in a lesson I taught to a group of 1st and 2nd graders in the Fire Island School District in New York, I used the learning target and success criteria, which the teacher had posted as an anchor chart, at various points during the lesson. Students were working on a unit of study titled "How the World Works," which involved investigating how products are made and goods are transported. The learning target focused on two lifelong practices of readers and writers that are identified in the New York State Next Generation English Language Arts Learning Standards (NYSED, 2017a):

- Readers think, write, speak, and listen to understand.
- Writers write for multiple purposes, to learn and for pleasure.

Figure 2.4 shows an abbreviated transcript of the lesson that illustrates how the learning target and success criteria were integrated into the student activities.

While students were learning about how goods are made and products are transported, the emphasis of the lesson was on the practices: lifelong readers write to make sense of what they read, and writers write for different purposes. Students also had a cognitive tool to use whenever they are asked to write about their reading because the lesson used success criteria as part of the learning target.

Cross-Disciplinary Practices

The careful analysis of practices in individual subject areas leads to greater understanding of how practices overlap from one discipline to the next. This understanding is particularly important at the elementary-school level, where the same teacher provides

Figure 2.4

SAMPLE LESSON USING A LEARNING TARGET AND SUCCESS CRITERIA

Learning Target:
I can write a response in which I retell details from the text by

• Identifying the book that I read;
• Explaining what happened in the beginning, middle, and end;
• Using transition words such as *first*, *then*, *next*, and *finally*.

Minilesson:

1. Today we will learn how we can use writing to help us better understand what we listen to and what we read. Let's read the learning target and success criteria together.

2. We are going to use our learning target and success criteria to learn more about how products are made and goods are transported. We are going to try out our success criteria after watching a video about how crayons are made.

3. I wrote this description of how crayons are made after I saw the video. How do I include the success criteria? What would you suggest I do to include more of the success criteria?

    In the video, I learned how a crayon is made. Rail cars bring wax to the factory twice a week. Workers mix in color. The wax is poured into a mold with lots of holes. The extra wax is scraped off and the crayons are pushed up through the holes. Labels are put on the crayons and sent to a machine that puts the crayons into boxes.

4. Together let's revise my writing to include transitions so we can better understand what happened first, next, and last.

5. Can someone read the revised response to the class? How does it help us to understand what we saw in the video?

6. Now you are going to practice how to write a response to help you understand what you read. You are going to read an article that you have read before about how oranges get from the tree to you. Let's look at our success criteria. How do you think you should begin? What else should you think about while you write? How can you use the anchor chart as you write?

Work Session:

1. Sometimes we need time to think before we get started. We are going to have five minutes of quiet work time. At your desk you have three cards. Use the green card when you are ready to start writing, the yellow card when you are still thinking, the red card if you are writing down a question you will need to have answered when the think time is over. I am going to be thinking and then writing as well.

2. When I see you are ready and have your green cards out, I am going to come to each of you and have a 2- to 3- minute conference about your work.

(continued)

Figure 2.4 (*continued*)

SAMPLE LESSON USING A LEARNING TARGET AND SUCCESS CRITERIA

Conference questions:
- *What have you learned about perseverance that will help you to get started? How can it keep you going?*
- *How can you use the success criteria to help you write your response?*
- *Where is the information in the text? Can you tell me that in your own words?*
- *How can you use the model if you get stuck?*
- *What have you learned about mindfulness that will help you if you feel stuck?*

3. Now that our work and conference time is ending, I would like your help in checking my work for the success criteria. I am going to take some notes while you give me feedback on my work so I can revise it later.
4. Before you finish your work time, I want you to check your work using the success criteria and make any revisions that you need.

Share time:
We are going to end today's class by sharing how using the success criteria was helpful in writing about what you read.

---

instruction in all disciplines. For example, science, social studies, English language arts, and mathematics all identify a practice that calls for students to use evidence to construct explanations. The following learning activities show how students can use this practice in different contexts.

In a primary-level science lesson, students examine images of different animals and their young to make observations. They sort the images to show how adult animals are similar to their young. They then re-sort the images to show how adult animals are different from young animals of different species. Students share their observations referencing specific details from the images, using the sentence frame "I think... because I saw..." as a way to make a connection between their evidence and their conclusion.

The same students are also asked to gather, interpret, and use evidence including art and photographs, artifacts, oral histories, maps, and graphs in social studies (NYSED, 2017b). Students can apply what they learned from the science lesson when examining different sources to draw conclusions in social studies. For example, in a learning experience where students are asked to draw conclusions about childhood in the past and present, they now know they can examine photos for evidence of how children from different time periods are similar to and different from each other. The teacher may ask students to sort the images, or the children may choose to do so themselves. What is most important is that students are using the details they notice in the images as the evidence to support their conclusions.

Students also rely on this practice in mathematics when they use evidence for constructing arguments and critiquing the reasoning of others. Students use bundles of 10 as evidence to support their thinking and explanations of teen numbers. In English language arts, students use what they notice about the characters, plot, and setting to draw conclusions about what is happening in a story and why. Students learn to transfer strategies when the teacher brings their attention to a core practice that they can use across disciplines.

Although students at the middle and high school levels traditionally attend discipline-specific classes, they too can benefit from the identification of core practices. For example, all four disciplines include a practice that requires students to analyze and interpret information. In science, the practice of "analyzing and interpreting information" requires the organization and interpretation of data through tabulation, graphing, and statistical analysis in order to make meaning from it and use it as evidence. Here is an example of a task that calls for students to apply this practice:

> Students determine the health of a local pond to make recommendations at a local town hall meeting as to what steps are necessary to preserve the pond or reverse adverse effects of the past. Students assess the presence of pollutants in the water by conducting their own tests and compare their data to data collected over the last five years from other organizations. They use the data as evidence for their recommendation during their presentation.

The statistical analysis skills that students learn in science are also an integral part of the mathematics standards and a necessary component of the math practice "construct viable arguments and critique the reasoning of others." When students are presented with different scenarios in which to apply statistical analysis, they must analyze and interpret the data, taking into account the context from which the data arose, before using the data as plausible evidence. These skills carry over to social studies and English language arts when students analyze and interpret various primary and secondary sources, considering the author, purpose, audience, and the context in which the source was written. Having the practice labeled and applied in all core classes leads to the understanding of how analyzing and interpreting information is a useful practice to construct meaning from a variety of sources and to ultimately use that information as evidence, regardless of the content area in which it is learned.

Summing Up

A curriculum that matters strategically incorporates practices to maximize learning both within and across disciplines. It emphasizes how, like the scientists, mathematicians, historians, artists, and other experts in the field, students can make sense of and apply what they are learning in new and unique ways. When practices are a priority, they are embedded into a curriculum document that identifies the practices that will be taught and assessed in each unit and that provides students with the opportunity to use the practices in a curriculum-embedded performance assessment. Students are made aware of practices because they are clearly named and communicated through a learning target and success criteria. Students benefit when practices are used across disciplines to learn.

CHAPTER REFLECTION

Use the following chart to help you reflect on how your school or classroom incorporates the tools, strategies, or practices shared throughout the chapter.

Practice: The application of an idea, a belief, or a method to construct understanding; often associated with specific disciplines but frequently applicable across disciplines.

Curriculum Reflection Questions:

1. Are the teachers who are implementing the curriculum familiar with the practices?
2. Are the practices that are taught and assessed identified in the unit of study?
3. Do students have opportunities for engaging in authentic tasks as practitioners using discipline-specific practices?
4. Are practices included as part of the assessment plan?

Strengths, Needs, and Possible Next Steps

Instruction Questions:

1. Are practices communicated to students through learning targets?
2. Are learning activities strongly aligned to the learning targets?
3. Do students use learning targets and success criteria during the lesson or reflect on them at the end of the lesson?
4. Are practices used across disciplines to support student learning?

Strengths, Needs, and Possible Next Steps

Deep Thinking

What does it mean to think?

People have pursued this essential question throughout human history. Entire fields of science are devoted to some aspect of thinking, beginning with philosophy and continuing with newer fields of study such as cognitive science. A quick internet search reveals the existence of many types of thinking and different ways to describe thinking. The question's importance is well known to schools, as seen through their efforts to incorporate this vast body of information and variety of approaches to teaching deep thinking.

Deep thinking occurs when thinking moves beyond surface-level understanding of an idea, content, knowledge, or information to the ability to relate, extend, or transfer that knowledge (Hattie, 2017). In this chapter, it is the overarching term for the kind of thinking students use to engage in multistep, complex tasks that require different levels of cognition and knowledge.

The chapter examines how to create tasks that engage students in deep thinking and explores how to link classroom instruction to the cognitive demand of these tasks. It explores design thinking and creative thinking, and their related instructional practices, as illustrations of deep thinking at work in the classroom.

What Is Deep Thinking?

To begin to address deep thinking in the curriculum and in daily instruction, schools must clearly articulate what it means to think deeply in a way that the teachers, the students, and the community can understand and use.

Guided by Superintendent Deborah O'Connell, teachers in the Croton-Harmon Union Free School District in New York created rubrics for grades kindergarten through 12, focused on key areas of their "Portrait of a Graduate" (Battelle for Kids, 2018). One set of these rubrics focused on critical thinking. Figure 3.1 shows the rubric for grades 9 through 12. Each dimension of the rubric identifies an essential element of critical thinking—cognition, strategy, perspective, and justification—communicating how the high school defines critical thinking. The descriptors at each level provide information about what critical thinking looks like in student work. The rubric is set up to convey deep thinking as a progression, providing all students with an entry point into the process and guidelines for moving from one level to the next. With a clear and common understanding of critical thinking, teachers were able to design tasks aligned to the type of deep thinking outlined in their rubric.

In New York's Fire Island School District, I have worked with Superintendent Loretta Ferraro to use feedback from teachers to design professional development that examines best practices in instruction and assessment. Their recent work has included an examination of deep thinking. Teachers Marialaina Appell, Jeanene Crawson, Bianca Daidone, Gabrielle Donovan, Colleen Ferry, Karen McNulty, Shannon Rickard, and Philip Tamberino engaged in deep thinking themselves by investigating and trying out different strategies in their classrooms. Their experiences guided their development of a definition and criteria (see Figure 3.2) that they could use to plan learning experiences for their students.

Figure 3.1

EXAMPLE OF A CRITICAL THINKING RUBRIC FOR HIGH SCHOOL

Critical Thinking Elements	Descriptors			
	Emerging	Developing	Demonstrating	Excelling
Cognition: Utilization of higher-order critical thinking skills.	The student demonstrates a literal understanding of ideas by **retelling** information. The student needs support to effectively express his/her reasoning.	The student demonstrates an understanding of ideas primarily through **summarizing or paraphrasing** information. The student attempts to effectively share his/her reasoning but requires prompting for further clarification.	The student displays a comprehensive understanding of ideas by effectively **interpreting, applying,** and/or **analyzing** information. The student includes a valid explanation of his/her reasoning.	The student displays a profound level of understanding of ideas by **analyzing, evaluating,** and **synthesizing** information. The student shares an original and compelling explanation of his/her reasoning.
Strategy: Ability to effectively plan, organize, and execute a plan.	The student attempts to solve a problem by posing **literal questions** related to the content. The student **begins** to develop and implement a plan independently.	The student **poses relevant and specific questions** to help identify the problem. The student **begins to demonstrate effective planning strategies to reach a solution.**	The student **poses relevant and high-order thinking questions** as a means to help identify the problem. The student **effectively implements a plan to solve it.**	The student **poses high-order, self-generated questions** to identify the problem. The student **generates various plans of action to solve it. The student has planned for possible revisions** that may need to be taken along the way in order to reach the solution.

Perspective: Understanding of personal thinking possible bias that exists, as well as varying points of view.	The student's ideas are **a restatement of others' thinking**. The student **understands that bias exists** and is working toward identifying where it can be seen within certain information and ideas.	The student's ideas exhibit **primarily original thinking**. The student is **beginning to identify existing bias** in information and ideas.	The student's **ideas exhibit original thinking**. The student **identifies existing bias** in information and ideas as a means of **acknowledging** and considering opposing views.	The student **elaborates on his/her original thinking** and ideas. The student **considers the existing bias** in information and ideas as a means of **thoughtfully examining** opposing views.
Justification: Use of relevant and accurate evidence to support original thinking.	The student provides **opinion-based statements** or biased information to support his/her thinking.	The student provides **evidence that is related** to the content to support his/her thinking and problem solving.	The student provides the **most relevant and accurate evidence** to support his/her thinking and problem solving. The student also demonstrates an **understanding of opposing points of views**.	The student **seamlessly incorporates the most compelling and accurate evidence** to support his/her thinking and problem solving. The student also demonstrates a **keen understanding of the various points of view.**

Source: Croton-Harmon Union Free School District, Croton-on-Hudson, NY. Used with permission.

Figure 3.2

EXAMPLE OF A DISTRICT DEFINITION OF DEEP THINKING

Deep thinking is a sustained process that leads to understanding. It occurs on a continuum that moves from an initial or superficial understanding to one that is analytical and well thought out. It requires practice and application and ongoing reflection that leads to an internalized understanding. When students engage in deep thinking, they

- **Reason** by using different skills, such as questioning, making connections, making observations and inferences, drawing conclusions, classifying and using patterns, visualizing and imagining, and evaluating and reconciling multiple perspectives/opinions and ideas.
- **Engage in metacognition** by seeking clarification, rethinking, reflecting, and revising.
- **Demonstrate growth mindset** through a willingness to engage in productive struggle and exhibit perseverance.
- **Demonstrate independence and autonomy** by taking ownership of their work but knowing when and how to work with others and ask for assistance and by making inferences.

Curriculum Through the Lens of Deep Thinking

Examining how these two schools define deep thinking provides insight into how deep thinking should be incorporated into the curriculum. Essential to both schools' definition is "thinking demand"—what type of thinking students will use and how they will use it. The Croton-Harmon rubric explicitly labels *cognition* as one of its dimensions, whereas Fire Island uses the term *reason* to describe similar thinking processes. Students must have tasks that require that they use different levels of thinking (cognition, reasoning) to engage in deep thinking.

Curriculum-embedded performance assessments (explained in detail in Chapter 2) provide students with the opportunity to use different levels of thinking. The design of a curriculum-embedded performance assessment begins with the articulation of the essential question and big idea.

Essential Questions and Curriculum-Embedded Performance Assessments

Essential questions, like the one at the start of this chapter, are large, global questions that can be explored and contemplated, elicit multiple perspectives, and do not have one correct answer. They are designed to provide direction for student inquiry and curiosity, and they lead to understanding that has been articulated through the "big idea," also referred to as an "enduring understanding" (Wiggins & McTighe, 2005). Together, the essential question and the big idea communicate the purpose and most important understanding of a unit of study, as in this example:

> **Essential Question:** What is the art of communication?

> **Big Idea:** Students understand that people communicate in different ways depending on who they are, where they live, and their cultural norms.

The essential question and the big idea naturally lend themselves to deep thinking by setting a context for learning. The curriculum-embedded performance assessment is specifically designed to explore the essential question and deepen understanding of the big idea. Notice in Figure 3.3 how the task changes when the essential question and big idea are revised to focus on concepts that transcend disciplines and allow for multiple entry points into their examination.

Students can continuously deepen their understanding of concepts and content by responding to the essential question repeatedly throughout the unit. They can begin a unit of study by writing and sharing their initial responses. For example, in a unit that explores the question *What is the art of communication?*, teachers can use baseline responses to determine the instructional entry point. They can also determine whether students understand the phrase "art of communication," what modalities students think of in terms of "communication," and what types of examples inform their background knowledge. As students engage in the unit, they can add to and revise their responses. These checks for understanding help students to process their thinking, and they provide teachers with information that allows them to provide effective feedback and adjust instruction as needed. The final response provides evidence of what students have learned as a result of their experiences in the unit.

Figure 3.3

ORIGINAL AND REVISED VERSIONS OF AN ESSENTIAL QUESTION, BIG IDEA, AND TASK

Original	Revised
Essential Question: How do you address someone in Spanish?	**Essential Question:** What is the art of communication?
Big Idea: Students understand that there are different ways to greet and address each other in Spanish.	**Big Idea:** Students understand that people communicate in different ways depending on who they are, where they live, and their cultural norms.
Task: Students greet each other as they come into the classroom and during exchanges in class.	**Task:** Students engage in video exchanges with a student in a Spanish-speaking country. They record their conversations and review them to analyze how the native speaker uses phrases and gestures common to the region and reflect on how they, too, can incorporate those phrases and gestures into their own conversations. Students work between sessions to incorporate what they have learned into subsequent video calls. After several exchanges, students share what they have learned about communication methods as a class and compare how different Spanish-speaking cultures use unique verbal and nonverbal methods of communication. They use their new knowledge to create various media resources to welcome new families from Spanish-speaking countries into their communities.
Commentary: The essential question and big idea are narrow in scope, and the resulting task is limited to the classroom.	**Commentary:** The essential question and big idea allow students to explore communication through different modalities and perspectives. Although the primary focus is on Spanish-speaking countries, the essential question could be explored in different cultures and across disciplines.

Guiding Questions

Essential questions are supported by guiding questions. Guiding questions are answerable questions that focus on the concepts, skills, strategies, and habits of mind students will use in pursuit of the essential question. Consider the following example:

Essential Question: What is the art of communication?

Big Idea: Students understand that people communicate in different ways depending on who they are, where they live, and their cultural norms.

Guiding Questions:
- How do we communicate with each other?
- How do we adapt the way we communicate based on context, purpose, and audience?
- How does bias influence our views about the way people communicate and our interactions with those who speak a different language?
- How does communicating in another language help us to deepen our understanding and appreciation for other cultures?

The guiding questions scaffold the learning that will occur in a unit and identify the different types of thinking students will use as they engage in the performance assessment. In this case, students are examining modality and methods of communication, considering the social and emotional elements of communication, and analyzing the relationship between culture and language. The guiding questions help teachers plan learning activities for the unit and adjust instruction based on student responses.

Determining Levels of Thinking

It is easy to assume that a task requires different levels of thought, but the best way to easily assess the level of thinking, or cognitive demand, is to use a research-based framework or tool. Frameworks help teachers determine the thinking level of tasks, revise tasks so that they demand higher levels of thinking, and ensure that instruction includes specific strategies for engaging in the thinking demands of the task.

One of the best-known frameworks used by educators to conceptualize higher-order thinking is Bloom's taxonomy. Most educators are familiar with the cognitive-process dimension that presents a hierarchy of thinking: remember, understand, apply, analyze, evaluate, and create. A knowledge dimension was added in a revision of the taxonomy in 2001. This dimension identifies different levels of knowledge that students use while engaged in cognition: factual, conceptual, procedural, and metacognitive. The matrix in Figure 3.4 provides a good way to visualize the dual taxonomy.

Figure 3.4

BLOOM'S TAXONOMY TABLE

The Knowledge Dimension	The Cognitive Process Dimension					
	1 Remember	2 Understand	3 Apply	4 Analyze	5 Evaluate	6 Create
A. Factual Knowledge						
B. Conceptual Knowledge						X
C. Procedural Knowledge						
D. Metacognitive Knowledge						

Source: From *A Taxonomy for Learning, Teaching, and Assessing: A Revision of Bloom's Taxonomy of Educational Objectives* (p. 28), by L. W. Anderson and D. R. Krathwohl (Eds.), 2001, New York: Longman. Copyright 2001 by Addison Wesley Longman.

Bloom's taxonomy is a useful tool for examining standards or practices because it offers detailed information about the level of thinking required and the type of information used in the process. For example, let's look at the following social studies practice:

Civic Participation: Fulfill social and political responsibilities associated with citizenship in a democratic society and an interdependent global community by developing awareness of or engaging in the political process.

"Engaging in the political process" taps into the cognitive process of "create." According to the taxonomy, a person creates when using information in new or novel ways. To fully apply this practice, students need to use their understanding of citizenship to create and carry out a plan of action for engaging in the political process. Citizenship is an example of conceptual knowledge because it is multifaceted and involves understanding the relationship between people and the place where they live, as well as formal and informal civic duties and responsibilities. The X in Figure 3.4 shows the thinking demand (cognitive process, column 6) and the knowledge demand (conceptual knowledge, row B) of the practice. Tracking multiple outcomes for a task provides educators with information about the scope of thinking demand and knowledge students will use throughout the unit.

Making a Connection Back to Practices

In examining curriculum through the lens of deep thinking, the goal is not to add more but to evaluate the level of thinking required by the outcomes, questions, tasks, and activities. This process begins by analyzing the standards and practices for a unit of study. If thinking is not part of these expectations, it is unlikely that the learning experiences will require students to think deeply.

Bloom's taxonomy is useful in evaluating learning intentions or questions because of its detailed approach to explaining different levels of thinking. However, only when we examine how thinking is applied to a task do we have a clear understanding of deep thinking.

Consider the following task:

> Students read a text to identify the steps in how a bill becomes a law and draw a diagram that illustrates the process.

Students demonstrate understanding by working with content knowledge in a familiar way.

To fully engage in *deep* thinking, students would need to use the information in an authentic way beyond the classroom, as seen in this revised task:

> Students work in small groups to read and summarize a current bill under discussion in the U.S. Congress. They find, read, and analyze articles in support of or against the bill. They use this information to prepare and participate in a class legislative session evaluating the merits and shortcomings of

the bill. Students write a letter of recommendation in support
of or against the bill to their U.S. representative, using information from their research and class legislative session.

In the revised task, students move from understanding information,
to analyzing and evaluating information, to creating a letter of recommendation for an authentic audience. This process requires different
types of thinking. The revision also increases the alignment between
the task and its intended outcome: civic participation, the practice
identified earlier in this chapter. The alignment between the learning
intentions and the task is a key element of curriculum design.

Design Thinking

Design thinking is a nonlinear, iterative process that seeks to understand potential users of something, such as an object or a process,
challenge assumptions, redefine problems, and create and test innovative solutions (Dam & Siang, 2020). Its multistep process requires
students to use different types of thinking to consider and address
authentic problems.

One of the best-known approaches to design thinking comes out
of the Hasso-Plattner Institute of Design (commonly known as "the
d.school") at Stanford University. It consists of a five-stage process:
Empathize, Define, Ideate, Prototype, Test (d.school, n.d.). What
makes the d.school design process interesting is that it provides an
approach to ill-defined or unknown problems in a human-centric
way. A curriculum that uses a design process focused on empathy as
a way to identify and define a problem is setting the stage for other
important elements of a curriculum that matters: social and emotional learning, and civic engagement and discourse, which will be
explored in later chapters.

STEAM curriculum is a perfect fit for design thinking because the
impetus behind a STEAM program is the engineering or design process. Let's see how explicitly addressing the thinking demands of each
stage of the design process can increase the rigor of a curriculum-
embedded performance assessment.

Consider the following task in its original form:

Students will conduct research about an alternative energy source (e.g., solar, wind, hydroelectric, low-emissions fuels). They share how this energy source can be used to solve different problems through a poster presentation and a formal letter to an environmental agency.

Figure 3.5 illustrates how this task can be revised using the five stages of design thinking.

The revised task specifically incorporates the design process to engage students in deep thinking. In this task, we see that students use the cognitive processes of *analyze, evaluate,* and *create*. They *analyze* the problem of the windmills by breaking down the situation into smaller elements: the original problem the windmills were designed to solve, the additional problems that it could potentially create, the effect on people and the environment, and the concerns and feelings of those affected. The analysis occurs during the Empathize and Define stages. Students then *evaluate* during the Ideate and Prototype phases by generating possible solutions and selecting the one that they will pursue. They *create* when they design simple prototypes and then a model to share their final thinking during the Prototype and Test phases. Students determine the real-world audience who will benefit from their work and the best way to share the results. Students use higher cognitive processes for a real-world, unfamiliar audience, leading us to the conclusion that students will engage in deep thought.

The creation of a model is a key component of design thinking. Simple models visualize potential ideas and determine which is worth pursuing further. A more complex model is then developed during the prototyping stage. Modeling can easily be incorporated into classroom learning activities in many different ways. Its value, as explained by McTighe and Silver in their book *Teaching for Deeper Learning* (2020), is that it is a form of dual coding:

Dual Coding... takes advantage of two distinct channels that the brain uses for processing information: a visual channel and a verbal or linguistic channel. Working together, each increases the power of the other, making dual coding a highly effective way to enhance students' understanding and retention of what they know. (p. 83)

Figure 3.5

EXAMPLE OF DESIGN THINKING

Steps in the Design Thinking Process	Revision
1. **Empathize** to understand people within the context of the design challenge, asking questions such as *What is the need or problem? Who does it affect? How does it affect them?*	Students consider the proposed use of windmills as an alternative energy source for people living on Long Island. They read a variety of publications that describe how energy from the windmills will be used, how the windmills will work, and different perspectives about the positive and negative impact of the windmills on the local community. Students identify community leaders, community members, and experts in the field of wind energy whom they can interview to provide clarification on their research.
2. **Define** the specific design challenge you are trying to address in an actionable statement written in a humanistic way.	Students use the information that they gathered to identify what problem the windmill farms were intended to address, how the windmill farms were proposed to address this problem, and the resulting advantages and disadvantages of the proposed solutions. Students choose and define the problem they will focus on related to the windmill farm on Long Island for the remainder of their work.
3. **Ideate** possible solutions to the problem and identify 2 or 3 with the most potential.	Students select and use a process to generate ideas about alternatives to windmills as a source of new energy on Long Island or ideas for addressing the concerns of using windmills as a source of energy. They conduct additional research to determine which of their ideas are worth pursuing.
4. Create **prototypes** of the selected options.	Students create simple plans that illustrate their proposed solution to the windmill problem they have identified. They request feedback from previously interviewed sources and pursue additional experts in the field for advice on their design.
5. **Test** to refine prototypes and solutions.	Students select one of the prototypes to fully develop as a model. Students present their model and proposed solution to an appropriate organization or committee that they have identified during their research.

Models can be used to visualize both processes and ideas. A process is a series of steps that lead to an end. A model for a process, therefore, needs to represent movement. Examples include a flowchart to visualize how a bill becomes a law or a map to illustrate the process by which recyclable goods are collected, transported, and arrive at a recycling plant. The deep thinking that occurs in the creation of these models comes from the opportunity to manipulate and concretize information in a way that requires students to make meaning.

The concept of modeling as a means for representing ideas can be extended to visual and symbolic representations. For example, as described by Isabel Beck and her coauthors in *Bringing Words to Life* (2013), a key component of introducing students to new vocabulary is for them to define the word, use it in a sentence, and create a visual image representing the word. Another tool for teaching vocabulary, the Frayer Model (originally created by Dorothy Frayer of the University of Wisconsin), incorporates an opportunity for students to use visual images when providing examples and nonexamples, in addition to the definition and characteristics of the word. The words selected greatly affect the depth of thinking involved in completing the chart. The more abstract the word, the more students will need to think about how to best illustrate its meaning.

Creative Thinking

Creativity is the capacity to produce products or ideas that are essentially new or novel. The term applies to both processes and products. Creative processes focus on the thinking that occurs during problem solving and innovation. Creative products are the results of that thinking, expressed through different modalities: oral, written, visual, kinesthetic, and technology based (Drapeau, 2014).

Guiding students through the creative process can lead them to creative products and engage them in deep thought. Consider the following two tasks:

> **Task #1:** Students participate in a kindness campaign by creating buttons that they give to classmates engaged in acts of kindness.

> **Task #2:** Students create and carry out a plan that recognizes others for acts of kindness.

The first task limits the choices students can make. They choose the design of the buttons and the classmates who will receive them. The opportunity to create is limited to the button design.

To fully embrace creativity as a means for deep thinking, a task needs to include creative-thinking skills. These skills were identified through the research of E. Paul Torrance:

- Fluency—The ability to generate many ideas. The focus is on quantity so that quality ideas emerge from the options.
- Flexibility—The ability to generate different kinds of ideas. The focus is on considering different points of view, approaches, changes, improvements.
- Originality—The ability to generate a one-of-a-kind idea. The focus is on the unique or different.
- Elaboration—The ability to add detail or extend ideas. The focus is on expanding or developing an idea further. (Drapeau, 2014)

The second task has the potential for engaging students with all four skills. Figure 3.6 elaborates on each of them to see how they are used during each stage of the task.

Figure 3.6

EXAMPLE OF CREATIVE THINKING

Task Description	Creative Thinking Skill
Students brainstorm a list of ways to recognize people in their school or local community for acts of kindness during the COVID-19 crisis.	Fluency
Students examine the options, considering constraints of technology, social distancing, available materials, and other factors. Students add to or eliminate their options accordingly.	Flexibility
Students work individually or with a virtual partner or team to come up with a plan for how they will recognize an individual or a group for an act of kindness. Students post their ideas for feedback from the teacher and their peers.	Originality
Students use the feedback to expand upon and revise their idea before carrying it out.	Elaboration

In this task, we see students engaging in the cognitive processes of *evaluating* and *creating* in an unpredictable, real-world situation. Students *evaluate* the problem (how to recognize others for their kindness, given the constraints of limited access, technology, and materials), and they *create* a plan of action that they carry out.

A curriculum-embedded performance assessment that embraces creativity is one that allows for a great deal of choice. The revised task was written to allow students choice of action and audience. When it was further developed for implementation, it was applied to a current, relevant situation. Although students may have, in other circumstances, considered another audience for their work, the openness of the task allowed it to be adapted to address the current need within the COVID-19 crisis.

Some teachers may be uncomfortable with the level of choice involved in creative thinking. It is important to point out that allowing students the opportunity to create the pathway for their learning does not mean students are operating without any guidance or that the task becomes unmanageable. Teachers can help students to meet the high expectations of more creative tasks by establishing check-in points that allow them and their students to monitor progress. Creative thinking is an engaging way for students to think deeply about their learning.

Incorporating Deep Thinking into Classroom Instruction

As this chapter illustrates, deep understanding is the result of recursive and flexible thinking. Given the time that might be needed for this to occur, it may seem impossible for students to engage in deep thinking during a daily lesson. However, the following examples show that even simple activities, done thoughtfully, require students to think in different ways and to explore different possibilities.

An important first step in making decisions about learning activities that support thinking is to return to the standards and practices. As described earlier, analyzing the standards and practices using Bloom's taxonomy provides the teacher with information about the type of thinking students are using. The learning target shares this information with the students, and the learning activity provides students with a strategy or skill for engaging in that type of thinking.

In Chapter 2, I shared an activity in which students sorted images to show how adult animals are similar to their young and then re-sorted the images to show how adult animals are different from young animals of different species. This activity required students to make comparisons. Because it was tied to the learning target "I can make comparisons by determining similarities and differences," students saw it as a strategy they could use to meet a specific cognitive demand.

Sorting activities can also be used to address other levels of cognition. To illustrate, try the following example with a partner:

Directions:

1. With a partner, sort the materials listed in Step 2 into the appropriate "can."
   - Trash can
   - Recycle bin
   - Reuse bin

2. As you sort the following materials, discuss why you believe the item belongs in the trash, recycle bin, or reuse bin. Come to consensus with your partner regarding your decision for each item.
   - Plastic water bottle
   - Plastic bag
   - Plastic egg carton
   - Milk carton
   - Vitamin bottle
   - Banana peel
   - Sock with a hole in the toe

The task seems simple enough, but if you try it with a partner, you will readily see that it is not. This is an activity I have done with many groups, including 1st and 2nd graders, middle school students, and adults. Experience has shown me that people have many different opinions about what can and cannot be reused and recycled, and groups will find different ways to convey their thinking. For example, one middle school group "arranged" the cans far apart and put items in between. Their thinking was that an item such as a plastic bag could be reused for shopping until it tore, and then it would need to be thrown out. A group of teachers created an entirely new label: Don't Buy. They placed items such as the plastic egg carton in that category because it adds to the pollution problem. They suggested buying eggs in paper cartons instead.

At the end of a sorting activity, it is important to let the students move around the room to see how other groups have sorted the items and to ask each other questions about their thinking. Students can then reflect on how their own thinking has changed, if at all, based on what they have learned from examining the thinking of others.

The reasons that students provide for their decisions reveal the criteria that they use to sort the "garbage." Students evaluate the garbage through these criteria to determine its appropriate location. When tied to the learning target "I can use criteria to evaluate information," students see that they have acquired a strategy for approaching a specific thinking demand.

It is interesting to note that both the student and teacher groups who performed this activity asked if they could create a new column or a label before they began. Even though nothing in the directions said they could not, they felt they needed permission before trying a different approach. That in itself reveals how we often limit thinking in the classroom.

Creativity

Many of us have experienced brainstorming ideas as potential solutions to problems, with a facilitator recording everything that is said. We have also seen the initial list of ideas remain posted but with little exploration or follow-up. This experience may explain why many teachers have not used brainstorming as a prominent way to promote thinking in the classroom. However, when properly executed, brainstorming is a simple classroom activity that promotes creativity and leads to deep thought because it enables students to use the creative-thinking skills of fluency and flexibility. The emphasis, then, is not on the product, but on thinking deeply and differently about what they know and what they are learning and then using criteria to evaluate their ideas.

Following through with these three simple steps can change the way brainstorming is used in the classroom:

1. Use a starter to generate ideas. A starter can be a word, phrase, prompt, question, or visual that prompts the generation of ideas, thoughts, connections, and processes. The emphasis of this step is on producing many ideas.

2. Consider different ways for students to record and organize ideas. This can include simple lists, webs, index cards, or online whiteboards. Students can record their ideas using words, phrases, images, sketches, or questions. The purpose of this step in the brainstorming process is to make connections, which trigger and help students retrieve other knowledge and ideas and generate possible new ways of thinking.

3. Give students the opportunity to revisit their initial thinking to evaluate, add to, eliminate, and revise their ideas. After engaging in a learning activity that provides students with additional information, they should reconsider their original thinking to assess and revise it accordingly. Input can come from a variety of sources such as text, video, and data, and processing activities can include discussion and writing.

Let's examine two very different examples to illustrate this approach.

Example #1

Students use a Frame of Reference Thinking Map (Hyerle, 2008) for their study of erosion. As shown in Figure 3.7, they record what they know about erosion in the circle, what has influenced their understanding of erosion in the space between the circle and the square, and any questions they have about erosion in the space outside the square.

After completing the task independently, students share their thinking in small groups. During their discussion, they use a different color pen to add to their original thinking. Students then watch a video on erosion and the formation of the Grand Canyon. They use a variety of resources (texts and visuals) to create their own model showing how erosion shapes the earth. As students engage in the activity, they continue to update their understanding of erosion on the circle map, once again recording their thinking with a different color pen. At the end of the learning activity, students write an explanation of how their thinking about erosion has changed and what questions they still have about the process.

Figure 3.7

EXAMPLE OF A FRAME OF REFERENCE THINKING MAP

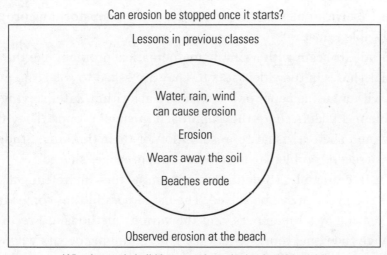

In this example, the initial brainstorming process occurs around the word *erosion*. It involves three questions: *What do I know? How do I know it?* and *What do I want to know more about?* The first question ignites the brain to begin the process of retrieving prior knowledge. The second question helps students to think about the reliability of their sources of information, and the third creates curiosity to learn more.

The initial thinking map serves as one organizer and the colored pens serve as the other. Students see their thinking evolve as they add new information or eliminate (by crossing out) what doesn't fit. Students solidify their understanding when they return to their maps and write an explanation of how their understanding of erosion has evolved and what questions remain that they can investigate further to deepen their understanding of the topic and pursue the essential question, Can man control the earth?

Example #2

Although educators might not associate creativity with mathematics, in her video on "number talks" (www.youcubed.org/resources/stanford-onlines-learn-math-teachers-parents-number-talks/), Jo Boaler (n.d.) shows how "mathematics is a creative and flexible subject." A number talk is a short discussion about possible ways to solve problems. It is a variation of the brainstorming process, applicable to math.

Students begin with a simple mathematical problem like the one Boaler shares in the video: 18×5. They are asked to solve the problem without using paper or the standard algorithm. After solving the problem, students share their approach in small groups. They then draw and share a visual representation of their thinking. Students solve a second problem using one of the approaches shared.

In this example, students brainstorm as they share the various ways the problem can be solved. The list of possibilities comes from the sharing by all members, and the various methods are recorded through the visual representations. The rethinking occurs when the students use a different method to solve a similar problem and share how their thinking about numbers has changed.

Summing Up

A curriculum that matters is one that routinely engages students in deep thinking. Students who engage in curriculum-embedded performance assessments pursue essential questions to develop big ideas that are conceptual and transferable to new and unknown situations. The curriculum-embedded performance assessments call for high levels of thinking and the opportunity for students to use their learning for authentic audiences and purposes. The creative process or design thinking provides additional pathways for engaging students in deep thinking. Everyday learning activities provide students with strategies for addressing different levels of thinking. Examples of such learning activities include innovations of sorting, modeling or visualization, and brainstorming.

CHAPTER REFLECTION

You can use the following chart to help you reflect on how your school or classroom incorporates the tools, strategies, or practices shared throughout the chapter.

Deep Thinking: A kind of thinking that moves from a general understanding of content, knowledge, and ideas to one that allows for application, extension, and creation of new ideas.

Curriculum Reflection Questions:

1. Do the essential question and big idea communicate the most important learning for a unit?
2. Does the curriculum use essential and guiding questions and big ideas to frame units of study?
3. Do students reflect on the essential question throughout the unit so they can see their thinking evolve?
4. Does the curriculum-embedded performance assessment call for high levels of thinking and the opportunity for students to use their learning for authentic audiences and purposes?
5. Are there opportunities for students to engage in design thinking when solving a problem?
6. Are there opportunities for students to use creative processes and products to develop new and original ideas or products?

Strengths, Needs, and Possible Next Steps

Instruction Questions:

1. Are students taught specific strategies for addressing different types of thinking?
2. Do students use criteria when evaluating information or ideas?
3. Do students engage in steps of the design process or creative processes as part of their learning experiences?
4. Do students participate in variations of sorting, modeling or visualization, and brainstorming as part of their learning experiences?

Strengths, Needs, and Possible Next Steps

Social and
Emotional Learning

The need to address the social and emotional well-being of students has been on the center stage in education recently for many reasons. According to editors of the *Handbook of Social and Emotional Learning: Research and Practice*, changing life conditions, increased economic and social pressures, uncensored and unsupervised access to media, and less overall social-emotional support have led to an increased need for social and emotional practices and policies in schools (Weissberg et al., 2015). It is even more necessary to address students' social and emotional needs as they deal with trauma from the COVID-19 pandemic, civil unrest, political polarization, and the challenges of an uncertain school year.

To have the greatest impact, social and emotional learning (SEL) needs to be attended to through schoolwide initiatives and classroom practice. Many have already incorporated separate SEL programs into school schedules. Although this is a good first step, it is not enough. To truly have a positive impact on student learning, SEL skills and strategies must move from being a separate program to an integral part of learning.

In turning the lens of curriculum to social and emotional learning, we will examine how schools can organize curriculum to help students view SEL in action in everyday life and, through naturally embedded learning opportunities, practice the skills necessary for their development as self-regulated, independent learners. We also will explore the need to address student mindset so they use these skills to foster learning and develop the forbearance necessary to overcome potential challenges.

What Is Social and Emotional Learning?

The most widely used framework for social and emotional learning is the one created by the Collaborative for Academic, Social, and Emotional Learning (CASEL). In a definition updated in 2020, CASEL defines *social and emotional learning* as "the process through which all young people and adults acquire and apply the knowledge, skills, and attitudes to develop healthy identities, manage emotions and achieve personal and collective goals, feel and show empathy for others, establish and maintain supportive relationships, and make responsible and caring decisions." The updated Framework for Systematic Social and Emotional Learning identifies five competencies:

- **Self-Awareness:** The abilities to understand one's own emotions, thoughts, and values and how they influence behavior across contexts. This includes capacities to recognize one's strengths and limitations with a well-grounded sense of confidence and purpose.
- **Self-Management:** The abilities to manage one's emotions, thoughts, and behaviors effectively in different situations and to achieve goals and aspirations. This includes the capacities to delay gratification, manage stress, and feel motivation and agency to accomplish personal/collective goals.
- **Social Awareness:** The abilities to understand the perspectives of and empathize with others, including those from diverse backgrounds, cultures, and contexts. This includes the capacities to feel compassion for others, understand broader historical and social norms for behavior in different settings, and recognize family, school, and community resources and supports.
- **Relationship Skills:** The abilities to establish and maintain healthy and supportive relationships and to effectively navigate

settings with diverse individuals and groups. This includes the capacities to communicate clearly, listen actively, cooperate, work collaboratively to problem solve and negotiate conflict constructively, navigate settings with differing social and cultural demands and opportunities, provide leadership, and seek or offer help when needed.

- **Responsible Decision Making:** The abilities to make caring and constructive choices about personal behavior and social interactions across diverse situations. This includes the capacities to consider ethical standards and safety concerns, and to evaluate the benefits and consequences of various actions for personal, social, and collective well-being. (CASEL, 2020)

Throughout this chapter, these five competencies will be the basis for our discussion of how to best align curriculum and instruction with social and emotional learning.

Curriculum Through the Lens of Social and Emotional Learning

Curriculum can address social and emotional learning in two ways: organizational structure and explicit use of SEL skills as part of the learning process. When themes based on the SEL competencies are used to organize the curriculum, human life, as explored in different disciplines, provides the fodder for both examples and nonexamples of the competencies in action. Students work with the SEL skills throughout the learning process, including in multistep performance assessments embedded in the units.

Organizing Centers

Students can gain insight into the five social and emotional competencies as they study people, places, and events. When units are organized around the competencies, the content provides a way to explore the *organizing center*—the central idea upon which a unit of study is built. The organizing center is communicated through the unit title, an essential question, and a big idea. Figure 4.1 shows the organizing centers for several units from a 5th grade curriculum and how they connect to the SEL competencies.

Figure 4.1

ORGANIZING CENTERS THROUGH THE LENS OF SOCIAL AND EMOTIONAL COMPETENCIES

Unit Description (Essential Question, Big Idea, Description of What Students Will Do)	Connection to the SEL Competencies
Unit #1: The unit "The Search for Who We Are" is organized around the essential question *What defines who we are?* Students come to understand the big idea that *through other people's stories, they can learn more about themselves.* As a culminating project, students conduct an interview with someone who they feel has an important story to tell. They decide the best way to share this story so others can learn more about the diverse people who live in their community. Students reflect on what they learned about themselves as a result of this experience.	This unit, with its focus on identity, addresses the competencies of *self-awareness* and *social awareness.* Students learn more about themselves by examining the lives of literary characters and real people.
Unit #2: The unit "Rights and Opportunities" is organized around the essential question *Do we all have access to the same rights and opportunities?* In this unit, students come to understand the big idea that *all people have the same rights in theory, but in practice, some people's ability to access the rights that are enjoyed by others is limited.* They read texts about the civil rights movement, particularly about the desegregation of schools and the continued fight for an equitable education for each student. As a result of this unit, students apply their own definition of equitable education and evaluate its presence in their school. Students identify ways to ensure better access and opportunities in various areas, such as the arts and STEAM, and present their finding to an appropriate audience, such as the principal and the school board.	This unit focuses on the competency of *social awareness.* Students examine equity and evaluate it within their own school community.
Unit #3: The unit "Respect" is organized around the essential question *How do we treat others?* In this unit, students come to understand the big idea that *all people should be treated with respect, kindness, and empathy.* Students explore bullying and how the decisions they make can affect others. They use their understanding to create a public service announcement that raises awareness about bullying in school with the intent of changing students' attitudes and behavior.	The focus of this unit is on *responsible decision making.* Students learn how the decisions they make about how to treat people can affect how others feel and view themselves.

As we learned in the previous chapter, the essential question and big idea identify the most important learning for a unit of study and serve as the basis for the design of the curriculum-embedded performance assessment. When the organizing center focuses on an SEL competency, students are not passively learning about the competency but engage in a task in which they actively explore it. The following performance assessment for the unit "Respect" (Unit #3 in Figure 4.1) focuses on the competencies of self-awareness and social awareness because it provides an opportunity for students to examine identity as it relates to themselves and the people in their community:

> In this unit, you explored the value of stories in learning more about others who have had different life experiences than your own. Now you will interview someone who you feel has an important story to tell that will show how people living in the United States have been affected by that person's experiences.
>
> First, you will write questions for an interview with a family member or friend asking about an important event or memory from that person's life that will help others learn about the diverse people who make up the United States and, in particular, your community. You can record or write the responses to your questions.
>
> Once you have completed the interview, you can share it with the person you interviewed and the community in a number of ways. When determining the audience, consider who would benefit from hearing this person's story. You can edit the interview to create a documentary, create a photo essay, use an app or program to create a book, or write a narrative. Whatever you choose, you will need to do the following:
>
> - Introduce the person you interviewed.
> - Provide background information about when and where the story takes place.
> - Sequence the events so they make sense.
> - Provide details to describe the events.
> - Provide a conclusion that identifies the importance of the story.

You will also complete a reflection that you will use in a class discussion. Your reflection should answer the following questions:

- What did you learn about the person that you did not know?
- How did the time and place of the events influence the story?
- How are you similar to and different from the person you interviewed?
- What did you learn about yourself?

In addition to focusing on an SEL competency, performance assessments provide the opportunity for students to *use* the SEL competencies as they navigate the extended task. Students need to make several decisions in completing this task: Whom should they interview? What should they ask? How can they share this person's story? To answer these questions, students need to employ self-management skills. Teachers can support students by embedding action plans as part of the assignment. In this case, students would submit a plan that answers the previous questions and includes deadlines for completion, thus breaking down the task into manageable goals.

Connection to Practices and Deep Thinking

In Chapter 2 on practices, I discussed the importance of authenticity. Action plans are another way for students to engage authentically in their work. The abilities to identify and carry out steps in an action plan, to sustain work over time, and to refine work based on feedback are all genuine components of professionals in various occupations. These tasks engage students in deep thinking as they work to analyze the information they gather during the process and make decisions about the best way to create products that share their learning.

Products created during each step of a performance assessment serve as formative assessment opportunities. A formative assessment is a check for understanding. When used effectively, formative assessments provide students with feedback on how they are doing while they can still use the information to inform their learning. The action plan, the interview questions, the write-up of the interview, and the draft of the final presentation all become opportunities for students to engage in teacher- or peer-feedback sessions. They also allow teachers to monitor student progress and adjust instruction based on trends and patterns noticed in the student work.

Curriculum-embedded performance assessments provide an opportunity for students to develop relationship skills as they work with their peers. In the interview task, peer-feedback sessions provide opportunities for students to interact in ways that support one another's learning. With other tasks, the group work is an integral part of the final product or performance, as illustrated by the example described in the next section.

A Middle School Example

At MS 45, Thomas C. Giordano Middle School, in the Bronx, New York, I have been fortunate to work with the principal, Annamaria Giordano-Perrotta, and her staff for many years. Our recent work has included a program to involve students in the school's professional learning sessions. During the first year of the program, teachers Kelly Martin, Jennifer Privitera, Raphael Trevisan, and Diandra Urena and their students examined how asking questions affects learning. Students were encouraged to generate their own questions in the context of learning about how human actions affect the health of the ocean and what can be done to prevent further damage. As a culminating project, students used their questions as the framework for a podcast in which they shared their findings about the economic, social, and environmental costs of pollution and outlined steps everyone can take to reduce their environmental footprint.

Students practiced SEL skills in the group work required to complete the project. The participating students represented grades 6, 7, and 8 and a wide range of background experiences (including English language learners and students with diverse abilities). Working collaboratively, they developed both their self-management and relationship skills. The task required them to be patient and take turns, negotiate roles, and reconcile their thoughts and ideas with those of their group. They needed to develop compassion to consider the needs of others when making decisions. The teachers coached the students through the process and modeled the SEL skills necessary for working together.

The benefits of this professional learning experience extended beyond learning how to interact with others and develop relationships. Students gained confidence and engaged in leadership roles within the school community. These added benefits illustrate how curriculum-embedded performance assessments naturally require and develop SEL skills, which can become part of practice when students explicitly name, apply, and reflect upon them.

Incorporating Social and Emotional Learning into Classroom Instruction

In addition to the built-in use of SEL competencies through curriculum-embedded performance assessments, SEL skills can be developed through daily instruction. Strategies include using texts and events as models of SEL in action, providing opportunities for students to empathize and appreciate different perspectives, and providing students with feedback and tools for self-monitoring.

SEL in Texts and Events

One convenient way to examine SEL skills is through the examples and nonexamples that students encounter in the texts they read in school. If we explain how a character's words and behaviors demonstrate the SEL skills and then label those skills, literary examples can prompt students to reflect on and monitor their own experiences, feelings, and reactions. For example, 3rd grade teachers Jessica Ning and Fazia Wellington, at PS 54 Hillside in Queens, New York, under the leadership of Principal Anita Prashad, designed a unit that explored change. As part of the unit, students read books to examine characters' emotions, how they changed, what caused them to change, and the degree to which the characters regulated their emotions. To help students identify and use language to describe emotions, the teachers incorporated the Mood Meter from the Yale Center for Emotional Intelligence (n.d.) into their discussions. In one lesson, students read *Thunder Cake* by Patricia Polacco (1990).

They used the Mood Meter to identify how the main character was feeling at the beginning of the story. As they read, they continued to track the girl's feelings, noting what was occurring that was causing her feelings to change and, as a result, how she felt at the end of the story. Students then used their annotated Mood Meter to discuss the character's feelings, how feelings are often influenced by events, and whether people can control their feelings or reactions. Throughout the unit, students continued to evaluate changing emotions in the stories they read, learning strategies for how to monitor their own thoughts, feelings, and actions.

This next example also illustrates the connection between SEL and literacy. It was created by educational consultant Elizabeth Locatelli for a webinar to help primary teachers with remote learning. It uses a familiar Winnie the Pooh story about Piglet's response to Pooh's Difficult Day. Following a read-aloud, students could engage in the learning tasks in Figure 4.2, with each step focused on developing both self-awareness and literacy skills.

Another way to examine social and emotional competencies is by examining historical events. One of my Adelphi University graduate students, Sabrina Davis, designed a unit that incorporates an opportunity for students to reflect on what they are learning about colonial America through an empathy journal. In the unit, students keep a journal with three columns. In the first column, students write their initial understandings of how the lives of colonists, Indigenous people, and enslaved Africans were affected by colonization. As students analyze primary and secondary sources, they use the second column to note the perspective presented, as well as new information and points that confront their own ideas. In the third column, students make connections between the perspectives and their ideas or to the world around them. Students reflect on how their opinions have broadened and changed by answering questions such as, How did the additional text present a different story of the same events and time period? How does empathy impact your understanding of the events and time period? How does this information impact your understanding of the desire of some to end celebrations and make appropriate reparations for the past?

Figure 4.2

QUESTIONS AND LEARNING TASKS
INCORPORATING LITERACY AND SEL SKILLS

Reading	Drawing	Writing	Discussion
How was Pooh feeling? What did Piglet do? Did it help? How do you know?	Draw a picture of yourself with someone who makes you feel good on a bad day.	Fill in the blanks: I like to _____ with _____ when I am sad.	What do good friends do for each other?
When have you felt like Pooh? How did you deal with it?	Draw a picture of someone who feels sad. Use details that show how you can tell he or she is sad.	Label the parts of the face and body that show sadness. Fill in the blanks: _____ is sad because _____.	How can you tell someone feels sad? What do you see?
Did Pooh think Piglet was a good friend? What words tell you that?	Draw and label a picture of something you miss doing with your friend(s).	Describe how you show your friend you care about him or her even though you can't be together.	How can you help a friend even when you can't be together?

The journal relies on texts that both the teacher provides and students research and choose to read. These texts need to include the voices of Indigenous people and those who were enslaved in addition to the colonists and early Puritan communities. They also need to provide modern-day historical accounts of these early events so that students develop an understanding of the origins of future patterns that would emerge in American history. When the texts offer different perspectives and the students are intentionally asked to reflect on these perspectives in a way that probes their previously accepted understandings, students are developing their ability to be empathetic.

Empathy and Appreciating Different Perspectives

The role of the empathy journal just described was to use texts and events as ways to learn about the social and emotional competencies.

It specifically focused on understanding perspective as a means for developing empathy. Another way to develop empathy and appreciation of different perspectives—important skills in developing social awareness and relationships—is through role-playing.

Role-playing is easy to incorporate into literacy instruction. Using role-playing in the classroom can begin simply by having students role-play different emotions. This activity not only helps students label and express their emotions but also helps them to develop their vocabulary. For example, students can work with a partner to act out words such as *pleasant, frustrated*, and *despondent* to develop variants to the commonly used *happy, sad,* and *worried*. The actors can select a word from a word bank, and the audience can use the word bank to identify the emotion performed. Once students become familiar with the vocabulary, the word bank can be removed.

Students can then progress to role-playing character responses in different situations. For example, books in a series such as Mo Willems's Pigeon books or David Shannon's *No, David!* offer opportunities for students to role-play appropriate responses to the different situations presented in the stories. This activity not only builds students' story sense through retelling but also develops their understanding of social norms and responsible decision making. Role-playing also provides an opportunity to model the traits of characters such as Elizabeti in the books by Stephanie Stuve-Boden. After becoming familiar with the character, students can role-play how Elizabeti would respond in different scenarios that they invent or that the teacher presents. In this case, students analyze a character and her actions as a model of how to identify and manage emotions, interact with others, and make responsible decisions.

Role-playing continues to be a valuable practice as students progress through school. Harvard's ABLConnect, a repository of learning activities, suggests role-playing as an active instructional strategy. It provides the following steps to guide role-playing as a learning activity at all levels:

1. Students prepare background knowledge to take on the role and understand the norms and expectations for participation.
2. Students partake in settings that mimic real-world situations in their dress, language, and interactions.

3. Students reflect on their experience, taking note of their strengths, challenges, and learning. (Weiner, n.d.)

Any topic, issue, or event that generates opposing views is suitable for role-playing as a way to understand different perspectives and resolve conflicts. For example, in a science classroom, students can select a current-event topic, such as groundwater pollution, vaccination regulations, or genetic engineering, and act as a panel of experts in the field, presenting their findings, offering arguments and counter-arguments, and proposing solutions. In social studies, students can role-play U.S. Supreme Court cases of the past to deepen their understanding of different positions on constitutional issues related to civil liberties. After role-playing past cases, they can then use their experience to offer arguments on constitutional issues they present to the class or those currently being argued in the Supreme Court, using additional evidence they gather through research.

Role-playing in these scenarios provides students with the opportunity to manage emotions, appreciate different perspectives, follow the norms of different settings, and collaborate with others. However, the power of the experience in developing student's social and emotional skills comes in the reflection that follows. Students need time to reflect on their use of the skills, what adjustments they needed to make in their own behavior, and what they learned as a result that will help them in different and unknown situations.

Connection to Practices and Creative Thinking

Curriculum-embedded performance assessments that align to discipline-specific practices, as outlined in Chapter 2, employ students as practitioners in the field. An added benefit of role-playing scenarios is that students practice the SEL skills they will use when they engage with an authentic audience and purpose. In addition, role-playing is an example of creative thinking, described in Chapter 3. It focuses on the skill of flexibility, the ability to generate and consider different kinds of ideas. Students examine different points of view and approaches to solving problems or addressing real-life situations as they role-play different scenarios.

Providing Students with Feedback and Tools for Self-Monitoring

Formative assessment is a widely used term in education. As I defined it earlier, it is a check for understanding; however, to have any impact on learning, it must include a response from the teacher. In curriculum, the most important formative assessment moments are those directly linked to the final tasks described earlier in this chapter. During these formative assessment moments, students should receive descriptive feedback from either the teacher or peers.

Quality written or oral feedback incorporates the following traits. It

- Connects to clear learning targets.
- Begins with strengths, includes questions or concerns, and provides direction on next steps.
- Is individualized and accessible to students in language, form, and length.
- Is provided during the learning process when it can still be used. (Lalor, 2012)

Here is an example of a learning target and the related work of one student:

> **Learning Target:** I can better understand the story by making a text-to-text connection.
>
> **Student Work:** *Lilly's Purple Plastic Purse* and *Julius, the Baby of the World* are both written by Kevin Henkes. In both books Lilly is a character. Lilly has friends named Victor, Chester, and Wilson in both books. In both books Lilly learns a lesson. In *Julius, the Baby of the World*, Lilly learned not to tease her brother. In *Lilly's Purple Plastic Purse*, Lilly learned a lesson about following the rules.

In this example, the teacher uses a chart (Figure 4.3) to provide feedback that is descriptive and actionable so that students clearly understand how they have met the learning targets and what to do to move to the next step. Not all student work requires written feedback, nor do all students need to receive feedback at the same time during the learning process. Students should be taught how to provide feedback to one another, and teachers can provide students with feedback as needed, with varying amounts of information. In this case, the decision to provide feedback to the student was based on the importance of the learning target within the unit. Students would be using the reading comprehension strategy to respond to literary and nonfiction texts as they prepared to create an online book, media, music, and movie resource for their class.

Figure 4.3

EXAMPLE OF TEACHER FEEDBACK

Strength:
+ You clearly state what the two books have in common; Lilly learns a lesson.
+ You identified the lesson in both books: Lilly learned not to tease her brother, and she also learned a lesson about following rules.

Question:	Next Step:
Why was this connection important?	Look at the chart we created on how text-to-text connections help us as readers. Use this chart to explain how reading the first book, *Julius, the Baby of the World,* helped you find the lesson in *Lilly's Purple Plastic Purse.*

Assessment-Capable Learners

Assessment-capable learners are learners who are in charge of their own learning and exhibit the following traits:

- They know what they need to learn.
- They understand who they are as learners and how to use their skills to achieve their goals.
- They are aware of how they are progressing.
- They know when and how to seek support in achieving those goals. (Hattie, 2012)

Students become assessment-capable learners when they consistently ask and answer for themselves the three questions presented in Chapter 2: *Where am I going? How am I doing?* and *Where to next?* (Hattie, 2012).

A Shared Experience

Earlier in this chapter I described the teacher and student learning community at MS 45, the Thomas C. Giordano School. In the second year of their program to involve students in professional learning, teachers Eric Agyenim-Boateng, Janice Cucciarre, Nicolette Grima, Domenic Scipioni, Matthew Springer, and Maryanne Zepata and their students focused on student assessment. Together they outlined the role of the teacher and the student in using John Hattie's questions as part of the formative assessment process. The result appears in Figure 4.4.

Figure 4.4

ROLES OF STUDENTS AND TEACHERS IN DEVELOPING ASSESSMENT-CAPABLE LEARNERS

Question	Student Role	Teacher Role
1. Where am I going?	Students take note of the learning target and success criteria for each lesson to monitor their learning.	The teacher uses a learning target with success criteria so students are aware of what they are learning.
2. How am I doing?	Students use feedback from the teacher or peers to revise their work or clarify understanding. When there is no formal feedback, students self-assess to determine how they are doing in relation to the learning target.	The teacher provides students with feedback, or students are given the opportunity for peer feedback or self-assessment based on the expectations established in the success criteria.
3. Where to next?	Students use feedback to make adjustments to their work and determine what resources or support they need to work toward their goal. When the students meet their goal, they begin the process again.	The teacher provides support in a variety of ways so students can achieve their goals. The type of support is determined by the student and can include conferencing, resources, or strategies.

As illustrated, the development of an assessment-capable learner occurs through a shared experience between teacher and student.

As Frey, Hattie, and Fisher (2018) write in their book *Developing Assessment-Capable Visible Learners,*

> Assessment-capable visible learners are cultivated by assessment-capable teachers.... Standing next to every assessment-capable visible learner is a teacher who is determined to foster these beliefs, dispositions, and abilities in every student. This teacher understands that her fundamental mission isn't teaching math, or reading, or science or any other subject. Job number one is ensuring that her students know how to learn. (pp. 10–11)

Connection to Practices

One way to ensure that classroom instruction focuses on practices is to make sure that the learning targets and success criteria that are shared with students communicate what students should know, should be able to do or be like, and the steps for getting there. As shared in Chapter 2, these learning targets and success criteria become the basis for the development of assessment-capable learners by providing students with the information they need to answer the question *Where am I going?*

Although students from the Thomas J. Giordano School were able to work with their teachers to reflect on Hattie's three questions, pandemic-related school closures prevented us from being able to meet again in person to reflect on their goals. However, after just one session of examining the role of these three questions in learning, students understood their value, as seen in the following quotes from their end-of-day reflections:

- I learned steps to take to know that I'm on track.
- I can use these three important questions to set goals for myself.
- I learned the purpose of having a goal, plan, and checking your work.

Feedback

An important part of developing an assessment-capable learner—a component that should be an integral part of any daily lesson—is feedback. As explained earlier, the perfect opportunity for providing students with feedback is formative assessment.

Not all feedback needs to be written. In daily instruction, formative assessments are more informal and fluid, and feedback comes in the form of a response from the teacher. As a result of information gained through a formative assessment, the teacher may provide oral feedback, regroup students, provide different texts, conduct small-group lessons, or provide different tools or materials for students to work with to achieve their goal. Without the response, the formative assessment remains little more than a missed opportunity to learn.

When students use feedback in any form, they develop self-awareness and self-management skills that allow them to use areas of strength to address challenges or needs and to seek assistance, when needed, to help them achieve their goals. Unfortunately, not all students are open to and readily accept feedback as part of the learning process, nor do they all have the stamina for maintaining the fortitude required of an assessment-capable learner. These realities explain the need to also address "habits of mind" and the concept of a "growth mindset" as part of social and emotional learning.

Habits of Mind and Growth Mindset

Both habits of mind and growth mindset are foundational to addressing the social and emotional needs of students because they move beyond students' skills to their belief in their own ability to learn. Habits of mind, as articulated by Art Costa and Bena Kallick, are

> dispositions of the mind that are displayed by intelligent people in response to problems, dilemmas and enigmas, the resolutions of which are not immediately apparent. The understanding and application of these 16 habits of mind [Figure 4.5] serve to provide the individual with skills to work through real life situations that equip that person to respond using awareness (cues), thought, and intentional strategy in order to gain a positive outcome. (Costa & Kallick, 2000, p. xvii)

Figure 4.5

HABITS OF MIND

1. Persisting	9. Thinking and communicating with clarity and precision
2. Managing impulsivity	
3. Listening with understanding and empathy	10. Gathering data through all senses
	11. Creating, imagining, innovating
4. Thinking flexibly	12. Responding with wonderment and awe
5. Thinking about thinking (metacognition)	13. Taking responsible risks
6. Striving for accuracy	14. Finding humor
7. Questioning and posing problems	15. Thinking interdependently
8. Applying past knowledge to new situations	16. Remaining open to continuous learning

Source: From *Learning and Leading with Habits of Mind* (pp. xx–xxi), edited by A. L. Costa and B. Kallick, 2008, Alexandria, VA: ASCD. Copyright 2008 by ASCD.

Look closely and you will notice that many of these habits of mind connect to what we have discussed so far about the elements of a curriculum that matters. The habit of "persisting" is evident in the Common Core mathematical practice "make sense of problems and persevere in solving them." The habit "creating, imagining, innovating" encompasses processes that lead to deep thinking. And the habit of "listening with understanding and empathy" is a necessary skill for developing the ability to understand and appreciate others.

The term *habit* is used deliberately to indicate the need for constant attention and practice. According to Costa and Kallick (2008), "A Habit of Mind is a composite of many skills, attitudes, cues, past experiences, and proclivities" (p. 17). The habits are built on the belief that "ability is a continuously expandable repertoire of skills, and that through a person's efforts, intelligence grows incrementally" (p. 7).

Habits of mind have both habitual and mindful aspects. When the desired behaviors do indeed become habitual, students draw upon them instinctively. For example, when a student recognizes that he is struggling with a math task and needs to employ a series of strategies, he has developed the habit of thinking about thinking (metacognition). He then follows a sequence of steps to work through the problem. These steps may require mindful actions such as rereading the problem, reviewing sample problems, or watching a tutorial; but the habit has been developed because the student believes that he has control over his learning.

Growth mindset as discussed by psychologist Carol Dweck (2006) also highlights the understanding that all students can learn:

> A *mindset,* according to Dweck, is a self-perception or "self-theory" that people hold about themselves. Believing that you are either "intelligent" or "unintelligent" is a simple example of a mindset.... People can be aware or unaware of their mindsets, according to Dweck, but they can have profound effect on learning achievement, skill acquisition, personal relationships, professional success, and many other dimensions of life. (*Glossary of Education Reform,* 2013)

Simply put, people who have a *growth mindset* believe that they can learn and grow when they practice and apply strategies to overcome difficulties. Those who have a *fixed mindset* believe that they either have a talent or they don't and that there is little they can do to change their capacity. Students with a fixed mindset see little reason to apply the skills needed to manage their emotions, understand different perspectives, and work toward achieving their goals.

Habits of mind and growth mindset focus on the underpinnings of social and emotional learning. If students don't believe that it's possible to have control over their learning and that all humans can continually learn, they may find it pointless to even attempt to use some of the social and emotional learning skills discussed throughout this chapter. Students need to be taught that they can learn, shown how to learn, and then given plenty of opportunities to practice. Letting students know about the habits of mind and growth mindset will help them work through the challenges of learning.

What does this effort look like in the classroom? Once students understand the two concepts and how they can be used, the teacher should incorporate them into daily instruction. One way to do this is by crafting questions and statements that cause students to think about their mindset and that require using the social and emotional skills they have learned.

Teacher prompts and reinforcements can guide students through the process of using the habits of mind and growth mindset. The first two columns of Figure 4.6 show examples of the types of questions and statements that teachers might use. Students can employ them as models for developing their own questions and statements, as shown in columns 3 and 4, to use independent of the teacher. Teachers can ask students to share their personal questions and statements so that others in the class can learn how to use habits of mind and growth mindset to learn.

Figure 4.6

TEACHER AND STUDENT QUESTIONS AND PROMPTS THAT SUPPORT HABITS OF MIND AND GROWTH MINDSET

Teacher Question	Teacher Prompt	Student Question	Student Prompt
Why is this challenge a good thing?	You can learn from challenges.	What can I learn from this experience?	This is hard, but that's OK because I can learn something from it for the next time.
How can you persist when things get difficult?	You may not have gotten it yet, but if you stick with it, you will.	What can I do when I feel like giving up?	I just need to stick with it. I just can't do it *yet*.
What can you do to overcome that difficulty?	You can do it! Think about how to apply your past knowledge to new situations.	What can I do that I haven't tried yet?	I am going to try this again in a different way.

Summing Up

A curriculum that matters provides plenty of opportunities for students to apply social and emotional skills to their own learning. Students learn self-management skills as they plan and execute curriculum embedded performance assessments. They identify and manage their own emotions to develop the relationship skills necessary for working with others, and in doing so, they become more aware of and appreciate those whose lives and experiences are different from their own. Daily instruction embeds examples and nonexamples students can use to examine and evaluate social and emotional skills in action.

A curriculum that addresses social and emotional learning includes formative assessment moments when students engage in teacher-student, peer, and self-assessment. Such experiences help students self-reflect and set and monitor their goals. For students to apply the social and emotional skills that will enable them to become resilient and self-regulated learners, they also need to be aware that they are in control of their learning. By examining habits of mind and growth mindset, students can come to understand that learning is a process that is open to everyone.

When a curriculum truly embraces the SEL competencies, students are aware of the relationship between their social and emotional self and learning.

Chapter Reflection

You can use the following chart to help you reflect on how your school or classroom incorporates the tools, strategies, or practices shared throughout the chapter.

Social and emotional learning includes developing an understanding of one's self to achieve goals, understand and appreciate others, self-regulate, develop relationships, and make good decisions.

Curriculum Reflection Questions:

1. Do units of study reflect the SEL competencies through their title, essential question, and big idea?
2. Do the curriculum-embedded performance assessments provide opportunities for students to explore the SEL competencies in the world around them?
3. Are the SEL skills related to social awareness, relationships, and self-management part of the performance assessment?
4. Are formative assessment opportunities included in the curriculum-embedded performance assessments and used to provide feedback to students?

Strengths, Needs, and Possible Next Steps

Instruction Reflection Questions:

1. Do learning activities use texts and other resources, as well as historical and real-life events, as examples/nonexamples of SEL skills?
2. Do learning activities provide students with the opportunities to learn about perspective? To develop empathy?
3. Do students reflect on their social and emotional skills as they employ them during learning activities?
4. Do students set and monitor goals to become assessment-capable learners?
5. Are formative assessments used to adjust instruction?
6. Are students taught about growth mindset and habits of mind? Are students taught to develop self-questioning tools and prompts to develop their own favorable beliefs about their learning and navigate learning when it becomes difficult?

Strengths, Needs, and Possible Next Steps

Civic Engagement
and Discourse

"Democracy is a method of realizing the broadest measure of justice to all human beings" (Du Bois, 1920). This quote from W. E. B. Du Bois is a reminder that education has a responsibility to support a sound democracy. It is through education that Americans are empowered to make decisions about their representative system of government. Americans have always understood this; it is the basis on which our educational system was founded. The critical connection between education and democracy has led schools across the nation to incorporate some type of civic instruction into their curricula, ensuring that students study how the government works and the rights and duties of citizenship. So, the question is not whether civics *should* be taught in school but the degree to which it *needs* to be taught.

In a curriculum that matters, the study of civics moves beyond the understanding of democracy and how it works, to civic engagement and discourse. The following definition describes the multiple dimensions of civic engagement and sets a context for the type of learning described in this chapter:

> Civic engagement means working to make a difference in the civic life of our communities and developing the combination of knowledge, skills, values, and motivation to make that difference. It means

promoting the quality of life in a community, through both political and non-political processes. (Ehrlich, 2000, p. vi)

Engagement is both a vehicle for civic learning and a result. Research shows that students who engage in civic activities as part of their education are more committed to civic participation in the long term (Gould, 2011). Studies have also shown that ensuring the opportunity for student participation is more likely to result in civic equality—the right of all people to easily engage in elections, advocate for themselves, and influence and create policies that affect where and how they live (Gould, 2011).

By practicing the skills of civic discourse, students develop the ability to successfully participate in conversations with those who do not hold the same view or opinion, to reflect on what they have heard, and to adjust their thinking based on a deeper understanding of the issues. Respectful dialogue is a necessary part of the political process and the basis for civic action. When students discuss issues of fairness, equity, or indifference that appeal to their sense of compassion and empathy or their feelings of injustice and helplessness, they are more likely to want to take action to address those issues. Such topics are often controversial. Students must be taught how to engage in conversations about controversial issues and, for those conversations to be productive, how to hear and respond to the views and perspectives of others.

The goal of civic engagement and discourse in school is to bring together what we think, how we express it, and ultimately, how we act upon it to truly embrace the ideals of democracy. As described by Bernie Ronan (2011),

Civic learning actually engages all aspects of the human person—the *head*, through thinking, judging, deliberation, and advocacy; the *heart*, through empathy and care for the beneficiaries of one's civic action, as well as through friendship with those co-involved in the public work; and the *hands*, through voting, acts of service, and collaborative political action. These three aspects can be viewed along a spectrum of skills development—a civic spectrum, which, taken as a whole, reveals how different dimensions of the human person overlap, interact, and develop through civic work and in the growth of citizens. (p. 5)

As we turn the lens to civic engagement and discourse in this chapter, we examine how to use curriculum-embedded performance assessments to meaningfully engage students in addressing matters within their communities that concern them. We also look at the role of civic discourse and media literacy in preparing students for civic engagement.

Curriculum Through the Lens of Civic Engagement and Discourse

Consider the following scenario: Students take a walk around their neighborhood looking for examples of people taking action to be responsible citizens. One of the things they notice is that people handle their pets in a variety of ways in public spaces. The students decide to research the responsibilities of pet owners and to create a community brochure about responsible pet ownership. Their research includes the following components:

- Visiting the local animal shelter to learn about the purpose of the shelter and what pets need
- Interviewing people at the dog park to determine how they take care of their dogs
- Reading books about being a responsible pet owner
- Creating questions and interviewing a local pet shop owner

After conducting their research, each student contributes a piece of advice on how to be a responsible pet owner, explaining why the advice is important for the pet, its owner, or the community. Student pieces are assembled into a class brochure titled "How to Be a Responsible Pet Owner." The brochures are made available at the local animal shelter, at the pet store, and in the school.

These students participated in civic engagement through a place-based learning experience. Place-based learning centers the community as the focus of student learning. This curriculum-embedded performance assessment illustrates not only how place-based learning leads to social action but also the capacity of young students to address social issues that they observe in the world around them. In classroom learning experiences, students explore the question *What makes a good citizen?* to set the context for their work. Through their experience in the community, students learn about the relationship between their actions and civic responsibility. This connection between actions and how they reflect the values of democracy is a hallmark of civic engagement.

Place-based learning is only one approach to engaging students in their communities. Service learning is another. Service learning is "an approach to teaching and learning in which students use academic and civic knowledge and skills to address genuine community needs" (NYLC, n.d.).

Consider the following examples of service learning:

- Second graders visit a local park and take notes on the strengths and weaknesses of the park's conditions. Students write a proposal and make suggestions to specific departments within the government as to how the park could be improved. They present their final findings and recommendations to a member of the city council. (Halvorsen & Duke, 2017)
- Students research mental illness among high school students and the type of support high school students need when faced with mental health challenges. Students compare their research with school policy and make recommendations to the school board for updating the policy. Students share the information they learned and services available to the school through a social media campaign.
- Students find out that a local homeless man is a veteran. After consulting with a veterans organization within their community, they organize a campaign to raise money to help the man with his immediate needs. Students continue to investigate why service members become homeless. They write to their state legislator to voice their concern and petition for more local services to support service personnel returning home.

Each of these examples, like the place-based learning example described earlier, are designed to incorporate three principles that are important to civic engagement and distinguish civic engagement from other forms of community interaction:

- Students engage in research to ground their work in deep understanding of an issue in their community (Kaye, 2004; NYLC, n.d.; Wolpert-Gawron, 2016).
- Students make connections between the work they do in their communities, citizenship, the principles of democracy, and/ or foundational documents of the United States (Gould, 2011; Winthrop & Heubeck, 2019).
- Students reflect on their community work to build understanding and empathy and foster personal growth and awareness (Kaye, 2004; NYLC, n.d.; Wolpert-Gawron, 2016).

These experiences show students how they can shape the world around them in powerful and respectful ways. However, the actions support instruction in civics only if the research leads to deep understanding of the issues (community responsibility, mental illness, and homelessness) and an understanding of some of the ways in which citizenship is demonstrated in the United States (proposals to council members, presentations to boards, letter writing to government officials). It is the reflective component that makes these experiences personally meaningful and builds students' understanding and capacity to be civically responsible. As Cathryn Berger Kaye (2004) writes in *The Complete Guide to Service Learning,* "Reflection is a pause button that gives students the time to explore the impact of what they are learning and its effect on their thoughts and future actions" (p. 11).

Teachers facilitate the reflective process by providing students with questions and prompts that encourage them to probe and question their assumptions, examine and challenge their biases, and deepen their understanding of the societal issues. By asking these questions throughout the learning process, students can monitor their journey toward becoming civically minded participants in a democratic society.

Connections to Social and Emotional Learning

Two important competencies of social and emotional learning that are intertwined with civic engagement are self-awareness and social awareness. As noted in Chapter 3, self-awareness includes the abilities to understand one's own emotions, thoughts, and values and consider how they influence behavior across contexts. Social awareness includes the abilities to understand the perspectives of and empathize with others, including those from diverse backgrounds, cultures, and contexts (CASEL, 2020). Simply put, self- and social awareness are the abilities to look inward at one's self and outward to others. The connection between the two is what drives civic engagement. Recognizing feelings of concern, hopelessness, or powerlessness in oneself can lead to actions to improve the lives of others. Diana Feige (2010) describes this connection eloquently:

> Compassion is both a catalyst for service and a transformative embodiment of service. If service truly is learning, then it is transformative. And yes, much of the time, compassion can be nurtured. *With immersion in varied, direct-contact experiences complemented by thoughtful, systematic reflection,* the transformation, in some cases, is dramatic; in others, the transformation is initial (a seed planted) yet tangible. (p. 55)

Student Voice and Choice

The passion that generates civic engagement presents the design-dilemma question: Who should determine the tasks? The answer lies in the purpose of civic engagement: to educate students to become full and participating members of our democracy. Democracy does not operate on preplanned events but rather is driven by authentic experiences, based on the current issues of the day. Because these experiences are unpredictable, they prompt and require student-generated questions and actions. According to Rahima Wade (2009) in her article "A Pebble in a Pond," the teacher's role is to "allow students to observe their school, community, and world and to see what emerges as their concerns" (p. 52). When students' critical consciousness is raised, they begin to recognize and act upon social issues that matter to them and to explore ways to improve situations they see as unjust and inhumane. Personal relevance is a strong motivator for school-based civic engagement opportunities and also a predictor of engagement in later civic life (Hess, 2009).

A unit of study focused on civic engagement should extend the democratic process by giving students a voice in identifying which social issues are most important in their lives. Students should be able to choose what they will study, how they will study it, and how they will engage in their local, national, or global community. This approach is possible when the curriculum is designed to allow for student voice and choice, and it can be accomplished by using an overarching essential question that allows students to select a problem and issue they wish to investigate as a class, in small groups, or individually. For example, the organizing center in Figure 5.1 offers a wide range of possibilities for exploration.

Figure 5.1

EXAMPLE OF A CIVIC ENGAGEMENT ORGANIZING CENTER

Unit Title: And Justice for All

Essential Question: Is justice guaranteed?

Big Idea: Students understand that the meaning of the words found in the Pledge of Allegiance are reminders of fundamental principles and values of American democracy and, as such, are sought to be embodied in all aspects of American life. However, differences exist as to what constitutes justice and to what degree there is a moral imperative to ensure that justice is served.

Is justice guaranteed? can serve as the essential question for the year, with different units of study exploring case studies, or it can be used to create a unit to ensure that proper space and time is devoted to the study of social justice within the overall curriculum. Under the umbrella of the essential question, students can be guided in crafting their own questions for inquiry and pursuing a course of action individually or in groups. Figure 5.2 provides an example of how students might individually examine the overarching question through issues of their own choosing.

Figure 5.2

EXAMPLES OF STUDENT INQUIRY

Unit Title: And Justice for All

Essential Question: Is justice guaranteed?

Big Idea: Students understand that the meaning of the words found in the Pledge of Allegiance are reminders of fundamental principles and values of American democracy, and as such, are sought to be embodied in all aspects of American life. However, differences exist as to what constitutes justice and to what degree there is a moral imperative to ensure that justice is served.

Student #1

Topic: Racism

Guiding Question: What is systemic racism?

Inquiry: I want to learn more about systemic racism, how it affects the way we live, and what I can do about it.

Student #2

Topic: Native American Land Rights

Guiding Question: Who owns the land?

Inquiry: I read about the court case involving the Dakota pipeline. I want to know more about the Native Americans who live there and brought the case to court.

Student #3:

Topic: Poverty

Guiding Question: Can you work and be poor?

Inquiry: I want to know why the minimum wage does not provide enough money for people to live on and why families often have to work multiple jobs to meet their basic needs.

Civic Engagement Across Disciplines

Although civic engagement requires an understanding of how government works and the role of the individual and groups to effect change, it also requires the analysis of issues from historical, social, economic, and scientific perspectives. For example, multiple disciplines can be used to examine the issue of poverty through the guiding question *How much money do you need to live?* Students will need to examine poverty through an economic lens, using practices related to mathematics to determine the cost of rent, food, utilities, and other basic needs, in relation to the amount of money earned by working a low-wage job. This same question can be examined through a sociological lens, examining how low-wage jobs affect other aspects of life, such as childcare and family well-being, or through a health lens to examine the impact of low-wage jobs on the type of foods accessible at lower cost and their nutritional value.

Unfortunately, many educators associate civic tasks with only a civics or social studies curriculum. When civic engagement is offered only in these courses, students are limited to viewing social issues through primarily a historical or political lens. Social issues that warrant civic action exist across disciplines in science, mathematics, health, physical education, music, and the arts. For example, scientists need to concern themselves with policy that creates the parameters for clinical trials. Art curators need to consider how to convey messages of social justice when creating exhibits. Civic engagement should be part of any student's experience, with pathways through the humanities, STEM, or the arts.

Although not designed exclusively for civic engagement, "capstone projects" and "passion projects" are structures that model how to provide time reserved for students to work on a project of their choosing. They easily lend themselves to different starting points and the natural integration of disciplines that occurs when people engage in civic work. Students, like scientists, mathematicians, artists, and other practitioners, can work on teams drawing upon their individual expertise to collectively address social issues. For example, the scientist can draw upon a writer's skills to present scientific or technical information in a way that is accessible to those outside the field.

Passion projects often appear at the elementary level, with a specific block of time on one day or a given time on each day set aside for students to work on their projects. Capstone projects operate the same way but differ in that they are culminating projects that bring together what students have learned over time. In their article "Seizing the Civic Education Moment," Tripodo and Pondscio (2017) explain that in civic learning, class time is generally divided between reading and discussing writings on government and citizenship and working on authentic projects that allow students to use what they've learned to make the world a better place. Students "end the year having used political theory to advance personal projects and with a basic understanding of how to navigate governing structures to realize specific goals" (p. 24). This connection to civic learning is the key to making either passion projects or capstone projects legitimate structures for approaching civic engagement in any classroom.

> ### Connection to Deep Thinking
>
> As we learned in Chapter 3, deep thinking involves using a variety of cognitive skills over time to complete a culminating, authentic task. This process is evident in the design and implementation of civic learning experiences. Civic engagement requires students to *create*—the highest level of cognitive demand in Bloom's taxonomy. According to the taxonomy, a person creates when using information in new or novel ways. Students use their understanding of citizenship to create and carry out a plan of action that engages them in the political process.
>
> In determining the best course of action for addressing a problem or social issue, students can use the creative thinking or design thinking process. Both provide a way for students to think about the problem at hand, identify possible solutions, and then determine the best approach for meeting their goal.

Classroom Instruction Through the Lens of Civic Engagement and Discourse

Discourse, simply defined, is the exchange of ideas. However, many skills are necessary to engage in discourse that results in new understanding and learning. Civic discourse is particularly difficult because the topics under discussion often generate strong opinions. These differing opinions are an expected and necessary part of the democratic process and, therefore, should not be disparaged or discouraged. Difficult topics offer an opportunity to teach students how to engage in hard, often-controversial conversations in a productive manner. As Diana Hess (2009) writes in her book *Controversy in the Classroom: The Democratic Power of Discussion*,

> The rationale for discussion in democracy as a way to build political tolerance only has power, of course, if there is a reason why extending

important rights to people who significantly differ from oneself (either on the micro or macro level) enhances the health, stability, or sustainability of democracy. While there is a plethora of reasons why political tolerance and democracy go hand in hand, the most obvious is that society without political tolerance is likely to enact policies that deprive some people of their right to influence the political agenda and to have an influence on what is decided. That is, there will be no political equality. And absent political equality, there really is not a democracy. (p. 17)

Discourse is critical to civic engagement. As a result, students need direct instruction and support in developing the skills it requires. Students benefit from clearly articulated questions, a protocol for discussion, and criteria for quality discussion.

Quality Questions

Throughout this book I have discussed the power of essential questions in crafting units of study and designing curriculum-embedded performance assessments. These same essential questions can become the focus of classroom discussions. As essential questions are big questions with broad implications, guiding questions (as discussed in Chapter 3) can be helpful in linking the essential question to specific text or content that feeds the discussion. The guiding questions do not need to be answered in order or explicitly addressed during the discussion itself. They are available to launch or support the conversation as it unfolds. Figure 5.3 shows examples of essential questions and supporting guiding questions that can be used for discussion.

Although these questions are formulated during the unit design process, additional questions for classroom discourse can and should be generated by students as they learn about social issues and problems and determine how to best address them through civic action. In some cases, the guiding question for discussion will come from a specific text or other sources of input. In all cases, students will need time to prepare for a discussion that is grounded in evidence. Later in this chapter I examine this practice further.

Figure 5.3

EXAMPLES OF ESSENTIAL QUESTIONS AND SUPPORTING GUIDING QUESTIONS

Essential Question	Guiding Questions
Who is responsible for the earth?	• How has human behavior affected different ecosystems on earth? • What do governments, businesses, or individuals consider when making decisions about how to use the earth's resources? • What, if anything, should be done to make sure these decisions do not have a negative impact on the environment?
Do we all have access to the same rights and opportunities?	• Is education a right? • What opportunities does education provide? Is education necessary for opportunity? • Do we have access to an education that is good for us and what we want to accomplish in our lives? • Do we have a responsibility to make sure that education is good for everyone?
Can one person change the world?	• What does it mean to persevere? • What is the significance of simple acts of kindness? • How can we make our neighborhood a better place for everyone?

Protocols for Discussion

In addition to having quality questions, classroom discourse benefits from the use of protocols. Protocols offer steps and guidelines that enable all students to participate in the discussion. Vilen and Berger (2020) discuss the importance of this in their article "Courageous Conversations for Equity and Agency." As they note, "All students deserve rich opportunities to develop their verbal communication skills, and it is an equity imperative for us to make sure their thoughts and voices are heard in school" (p. 40).

Teachers can choose from a variety of protocols, depending on the purpose of the discussion. The "6 Thinking Hats," originating from the work of Edward de Bono (n.d.), is particularly effective for exploring issues from different points of view before suggesting solutions or making decisions. Each student is given a hat through which to analyze an issue or evaluate a solution or an action. For example, as students consider a possible solution to address the concerns of using windmills as a source of energy on Long Island (as discussed in Chapter 3), they would examine the issue through the lens of their given hats, as shown in the example in Figure 5.4. I would recommend having students switch hats at least once so they experience the discussion from a different perspective. Wearing a variety of hats allows students to see issues and solutions from a perspective that would not naturally be their own. It opens the door for further research, discussion, and input on next steps.

The "4 A's Text Protocol" (SRI, n.d.) was designed for examining texts. Discourse is most effective when it is grounded in research. Discourse around difficult and controversial topics can decay into a heated exchange of opinion with no factual basis unless students have read and analyzed relevant texts before the discussion. The 4 A's ask students to examine text through these questions:

- What **Assumptions** does the author of the text hold?
- What do you **Agree** with in the text?
- What do you want to **Argue** with in the text?
- What parts of the text do you want to **Aspire** to (or **Act** upon)? (SRI, n.d.)

For example, in a unit in which students examine the essential question *Who has the power?*, students investigate federalism and the roles and responsibilities of the national and state governments. After analyzing historical events and constitutional cases, students apply their understanding to current events. They read several articles about the role of the federal and state governments regarding providing hospitals with ventilators and personal protection equipment, business closings, and school reopenings during the COVID-19 pandemic, and they discuss each topic using the 4 A's protocol.

Using the 4 A's protocol allows all members of the classroom to explore an author's claim in light of the students' own thoughts and ideas and leads to further examination of the evidence used by the author in the argument. However, although the protocol allows students to examine their own thinking, it does not guarantee that all members have an opportunity to voice their ideas. In this case, it would be helpful to add a participation protocol.

Figure 5.4

EXAMPLE OF THE 6-HAT PROTOCOL

Hat	Example
Blue Hat manages the discussion.	The student with the blue hat acts as the committee chairperson, ensuring that the group adheres to discussion norms, taking notes, and summarizing the conversation.
Green Hat presents possibilities, new ideas, and different ways of thinking about the problem.	The student with the green hat offers new ideas or points out possibilities and concepts that could be explored further—for example, smaller wind farms, other locations, tax incentives, or discounted energy costs for towns or individuals affected by the wind farms.
Red Hat relies on feeling and presents an emotional response.	The student with the red hat shares feelings that come from the suggestion under discussion—for example, nostalgia from those who prefer little change, relief from those who feel their voice has not been heard, added interest from those who could receive tax benefits.
Yellow Hat identifies the good—the benefits and the positives in what is being shared.	The student with the yellow hat points out the positive aspects or advantages that emerge in the discussion. These could include environmental benefits or economic benefits from a windfarm.
Black Hat brings attention to areas of weakness or concerns about what is presented.	The student with the black hat points out the faults in the suggested plan. These could include negative impact on the environment or perhaps choosing a location based on poverty versus privilege.
White Hat attends to the concrete details and facts that are shared and additional information that is needed.	The student with the white hat is responsible for determining how information the group has obtained supports or disputes the ideas shared and what additional information is needed to come to a decision. This information could be testimonials from those potentially affected, notes from town meetings, economic or environmental impact studies.

The "2-Cent Protocol" involves everyone in the conversation. Each person in the group is given two pennies. Individuals place one of their pennies in a center space after they offer a contribution to the conversation. After they have given up both of their coins, they cannot engage again until everyone in the group has used their pennies. Discussion mapping helps students to see the flow of conversation and exchange of ideas. An observer traces the route of the conversation on a simple seating chart so the group can later reflect on the level of participation of different group members and identify steps for more active and equal participation in future discussions.

Criteria for Quality Discussion

Establishing and reflecting on group norms or criteria is another necessary component for successful discourse. Students are much more aware of the criteria and understand their value in quality discourse when they participate in the creation of these classroom norms. Diane Cunningham (2020), in her article "Three Moves to Elevate Student Discussion," describes the following steps for establishing criteria with students:

1. Using sticky notes, students independently generate their own ideas in response to the questions *What does a good discussion sound like? Look like?* Individual student responses might include those shown in Figure 5.5.
2. Students work in small groups to cluster their sticky notes based on similar responses, as shown in Figure 5.6.
3. Students share out to the large group one of the criteria they identified. Before sharing out, each group selects their top three criteria so they are prepared in case of duplication.
4. Once all groups have shared, the class evaluates the list to see if anything else should be added.
5. Students examine other tools (checklists and rubrics supplied by the teacher) that have established criteria and take note of what might be missing from the class list.
6. Students revise the criteria based on the samples they examine to create their final list, as shown in Figure 5.7.
7. Students test their criteria during a small-group discussion, reflect on the criteria, and make any additional revisions.

The criteria are then posted and used during classroom discussions. Students reflect on the criteria following group discussions. They also reflect on their own participation. They set goals as individuals and as a group and monitor their progress for meeting these goals as they continue to engage in discussion.

Connection to Social and Emotional Learning

Students draw upon social and emotional competencies when engaging in discourse. They develop relationship skills by using protocols and criteria for discussion. Both provide guidance on how to engage in conversations that allow all voices to be heard and considered. Protocols such as the 6-Hat Protocol purposefully teach students to consider different perspectives, a key to developing social awareness. Students self-monitor when they self-assess their own participation and role in a group discussion, determine the strengths and needs of their groups, and set goals for both.

Figure 5.5

ESTABLISHING CRITERIA FOR QUALITY DISCUSSIONS: QUESTIONS AND STUDENT RESPONSES

What does a quality discussion look like?

- Referencing notes on text
- Making eye contact
- Facing each other
- Sitting in a circle
- Actively listening by leaning forward
- Being present and not distracted with pens, books, and other materials
- Nodding head
- Indicating thumbs up/thumbs down

What does a quality discussion sound like?

- Asking questions
- Letting one student speak at a time
- Building off the ideas of others
- Taking turns
- Summarizing
- Respectfully agreeing/disagreeing
- Using "I" statements
- Citing specific paragraph or page numbers
- Referring to experiences

Figure 5.6

CLUSTERING SIMILAR RESPONSES

- Eye contact; face each other; lean forward; be present and not distracted; head nodding; thumbs up/thumbs down
- Share my perspective/opinion with support; reference the text with page or paragraph numbers; connect my own experiences, if relevant
- Ask questions; clarify statements
- Agree or disagree respectfully; build on others' ideas; make connections between ideas; use "I" statements
- Pay attention to my group; stay focused and get back on track; invite classmates who are quiet into the conversation
- One student speaking at a time; taking turns; listening to understand

Figure 5.7

FINAL CRITERIA

- Stay focused on the topic and guiding questions, using text evidence and relevant experience to support your point of view.
- Be present and use nonverbal ways of staying involved in the discussion: eye contact, leaning forward, head nodding, thumbs up/thumbs down.
- Take turns, with one student speaking at a time, and listen to understand.
- Ask questions to understand others' points of view and to clarify information.
- Build on others' ideas and make connections between ideas.
- Agree or disagree respectfully, using "I" statements to voice your opinion.
- Pay attention to the group; help it to stay focused and get back on track, and invite classmates who are quiet into the conversation.

Media Literacy

Fundamental to civic engagement and discourse is media literacy. According to the National Association for Media Literacy Education, the purpose of media literacy is to "help individuals of all ages develop the habits of inquiry and skills of expression that they need to be critical thinkers, effective communicators, and active citizens in today's world" (NAMLE, n.d.). Media literacy requires the ability to access, analyze, create, reflect, and act using all forms of communication, whether they be electronic, digital, print, or artistic visuals (Hobbs, 2020; NAMLE, n.d.).

Throughout this chapter, we have reviewed examples of civic engagement that illustrate how to use media to create and act. For example, when students create brochures, they use both print and visual media to convey information about good citizenship to the community. In creating a social media campaign, students use different platforms with appropriate video, audio, slogans, and images to convey messages about mental health issues in teens. These and other forms of media provide options for students to create and act upon civic issues in ways that reflect who they are and that can best reach those who are part of their communities.

The analysis and evaluation of media is necessary for students to develop their own point of view, engage in civil discourse with others, and determine a course of action to address social issues. Without this ability, students may partake in uncivil online behavior; be manipulated to believe false, misleading, or low-quality information; and accept only those sources that validate our own perspectives (Collins, 2017).

Connection to Practices

Many discipline-specific practices (as discussed in Chapter 2) incorporate skills related to media literacy. For example, in social studies, students engage in inquiry that requires them to source and cite information and analyze how evidence is used to support a claim. In science, students obtain, evaluate, and communicate information (NGSS, 2013). Accomplishing these tasks requires making sense of information found in different multimedia sources and communicating in different media to share what they learn. The Common Core State Standards contain literacy standards for science, social studies, and technical subjects that apply reading and writing skills to media consumption and distribution.

In addition, there are many sets of standards that transcend disciplines and identify media literacy skills. These include the following:

- The International Society for Technology in Education (ISTE) Standards: These seven standards focus on thinking, evaluating, and producing information using technology. (www.iste .org/standards/for-students)
- The National Coalition for Core Arts Standards: These media literacy standards for creating, performing, presenting,

producing, responding, and connecting in the arts were developed by an alliance of arts and art education organizations. (www.nationalartsstandards.org/)

- The Teaching Tolerance Digital Literacy Framework: The framework specifies seven key areas in which students need support developing digital and civic literacy skills. (www.tolerance.org/frameworks/digital-literacy)

When identified during the first stage of the curriculum design process, these standards can help to ensure that important media literacy skills are taught and assessed during the unit.

For example, consider a scenario in which students participate in a Socratic seminar to discuss the essential question *Is climate change real?* Students must access, analyze, and evaluate different sources to prepare and support their argument during the debate. Doing so requires that students determine the point of view of the author, the author's credibility as a source, the quality of the message, and the potential effect of using the information as part of their own message. Students need to source each document, attending to details such as the date, author, publisher, purpose, technique, and context, to determine the reliability of the information presented. Only when they are certain of the reliability of the information they have gathered, have enough evidence to support their thinking, and have carefully considered possible counterarguments are they ready to participate in the discussion.

The Center for Media Literacy suggests these five core concepts and questions for analyzing media:

1. Authorship: Who created this message?
2. Format: What creative techniques are used to attract my attention?
3. Audience: How might different people understand this message differently?
4. Content: What values, lifestyles, and points of view are represented in, or omitted from, this message?
5. Purpose: Why is this message being sent? (Share, Jolls, & Thoman, 2005)

Questions such as these provide students with a cognitive routine for analysis that will benefit them not only in preparation for civic engagement and discourse in the classroom but also when reading or viewing media sources in their daily lives. Given the large volume of information available, the use of algorithms to determine what we see online, and the cognitive biases embedded in the way that we think, lessons on media literacy are a vital component in any classroom where civic engagement and discourse is the aim (Collins, 2017).

Summing Up

In a curriculum that matters, the natural audience and beneficiary of student work is the community itself. Students learn about civic engagement by selecting problems of concern, investigating solutions, and developing actionable plans to address them. Civic discourse is critical to civic engagement. When students discuss issues related to fairness, equity, or indifference that appeal to their sense of compassion and empathy or injustice and helplessness, they are more likely to want to take action to address them. Discourse is most productive when supported by high-quality questions, protocols, and criteria to guide the discussion itself. Explicit instruction in media literacy prepares students for civic engagement and discourse. Students learn strategies to select, evaluate, and use information to support their discourse and actions.

CHAPTER REFLECTION

Use the following chart to help you reflect on how your school or classroom incorporates the tools, strategies, or practices shared throughout the chapter.

Civic engagement is active participation as a local, state, national, or global community member. **Civic discourse** is the ability to successfully participate in conversations with those who do not hold the same view or opinion and to learn from the experience.

Curriculum Reflection Questions:

1. Do students have opportunities to engage with the community in meaningful ways?
2. Are students given choices about what they will learn, how they will learn, and how they will share their learning?
3. Are connections between the work students do in their communities clearly connected to citizenship and the principles of democracy?
4. Are opportunities for civic engagement available through different disciplines and pathways?
5. Is students' work grounded in research that helps them deepen their understanding of community issues?
6. Do students reflect on their work in ways that build empathy and foster personal growth and awareness?

Strengths, Needs, and Possible Next Steps

Instruction Reflection Questions:

1. Do students routinely engage in discourse that challenges their thinking and helps them to understand experiences, beliefs, opinions, and perspectives other than their own?
2. Do opportunities for discourse focus on meaningful questions? Are discussions guided by protocols and criteria?
3. Are students taught media-literacy skills that allow them to select, evaluate, and use information to ground their discourse and actions?

Strengths, Needs, and Possible Next Steps

6

Equity

When we turn to equity as our lens for viewing curriculum, we can see how strategically leveraging the other elements we have examined can provide access to high-quality learning experiences for all students. Following the suggested steps and the recommended instructional activities found throughout this book will likely result in positive changes for students, but doing so doesn't necessarily mean the curriculum is equity-minded. It is important to understand how the various actions—for example, using curriculum-embedded performance assessments, inviting students to coconstruct learning experiences, and reflecting on learning—are useful for designing curriculum to build equitable learning experiences.

The necessary first step for building equity through curriculum and instruction is to turn the lens inward. Those who design the curriculum—and the teachers who will use it—must thoughtfully examine their own social identity related to race, ethnicity, religion, disability status, class, and gender. The deep personal reflection around identity that is required of today's educators is essential and complicated. As a white woman growing up in suburban Long Island, New York, during the 1970s, my identity was shaped by my experiences. I was very aware of gender biases faced by girls and women and what steps they were taking to make decisions about the lives they wished to live. What I witnessed would shape the expectations I had for myself and my determination for achieving my goals.

It was not until I began my work in education that I realized how little I knew about biases around race, religion, sexuality, and class; how they influenced my actions; and what I could do about them. I remember how anxious I felt when traveling into the urban communities of New York City. I came to realize that my concerns were the result of stereotypes that had been repeatedly told to me my whole life. My experiences in urban schools with teachers of different races and ethnicities (particularly those who engaged with me in conversations about equity) and an examination of what was at the root of my concern led me to understand my thinking. This awareness helped me to change my perspectives and interactions, the way I structured professional learning, and the examples and models that I incorporated into my programs.

My own identity work has been a constant process of unlearning and learning, and one that is not complete. I continually read, discuss, reread, think, and talk some more to understand how my worldview was shaped by my experiences, recognize how this affects my life and the work that I do in schools, and to have a greater consciousness of the experiences of those whose lives are different from my own.

It is a lifelong journey that needs constant attention and requires deep reflection on my thoughts, words, and actions. Although highly personal, there are many groups, organizations, and online communities that can be supportive in this journey. Establishing a school-based book club on any of the references found throughout this chapter is a good way to start. Only through personal reflection can educators do the hard work of addressing their own biases to design and implement a curriculum that creates equitable learning experiences. Without doing so, educators can carry their biases into the curriculum, and it becomes more likely that students will be taught misleading, inaccurate, or harmful information about other people due to curriculum designed with the best of intentions. When curriculum designers commit to doing this work around identity, they can reduce the likelihood that the burden of attending to equity will fall on the shoulders of the lone teacher of color, or the Muslim teacher, or the teachers with a disability (J. Borgioli Binis, personal communication, November 13, 2020).

The importance of examining individual teachers' identity cannot be overstated. In a conversation about the impact of identity work with Charles Sperrazza, principal of PS 108, the Philip J. Abinanti School in the Bronx, New York, he shared the following:

> When educators make the commitment to the deep examination of their own identity and place in the world, they are making an investment in the lives of their students. The teacher's identity work, or lack of it, can either enhance or destroy a child's perception of identity.

Charles also spoke about the role of the collective school identity. As I noted in Chapter 1, the first way a school communicates its identity is through its vision and mission statements. Words, however, are not enough. Together, the leadership, teachers, and staff must send a message to students and their families about their beliefs through their actions. This messaging begins with welcoming parents and students and giving individual attention to addressing their needs, concerns, and questions. Each parent and child must be seen and heard. Conversations and decisions made by the educators in the building must center on the effect on student learning. Developing a positive collective identity and establishing a collective efficacy can have a profound impact on building and implementing a curriculum that attends to equity.

To help schools to build equity through curriculum, I identify the following five criteria based on research in the field of equity:

1. Curriculum and instruction honors students' cultural and experiential backgrounds and builds off their strengths and interests (Bryan-Gooden, Hester, & Peoples, 2019; Ladson-Billings, 2014; Saavedra & Nolan, 2018; Smith, Frey, Pumpian, & Fisher, 2017).
2. Students have access to and are held to high expectations (Hammond, 2015; Ladson-Billings, 2014; Smith et al., 2017).
3. Students engage in authentic experiences that develop relationships and build human and social capital and civic equity (Bryan-Gooden et al., 2019; Hammond, 2015; Ladson-Billings, 2014; Smith et al., 2017).

4. Students engage in their learning (Baker et al., 2014; Hammond, 2015; Ladson-Billings, 2014; Saavedra & Nolan, 2018; Smith et al., 2017).

5. Students become independent and self-regulated learners (Hammond, 2015; Smith et al., 2017).

In the remainder of this chapter, I unpack these criteria, restating each one with indicators of how it is evidenced in the curriculum. I show how each criterion has been addressed through the previous elements, what additional steps need to be taken to embed it in the curriculum and teachers' instructional practices, and why taking the suggested action is necessary for creating equitable learning opportunities.

Equity Criterion #1

Curriculum and instruction honors students' cultural and experiential backgrounds and builds off their strengths and interests by ensuring curriculum reflects the diverse experiences of many cultures and uses culture, experience, and different ways of knowing and understanding as strengths for moving learning forward.

At the core of the work being done in schools to center students' cultural and experiential backgrounds are culturally responsive practices. *Culturally responsive education* refers to the "combination of teaching, pedagogy, curriculum theories, attitudes, practices, and instructional materials that center students' culture, identities, and contexts through educational systems" (Bryan-Gooden et al., 2019). A curriculum that embraces culturally responsive practices centers groups and content that have been historically pushed to the margins by those in authority. Doing so means that rather than focusing on Black history only in February, the art, literature, and advocacy efforts of Black Americans are celebrated throughout the school year. Cultural experiences are embedded in all aspects of learning, not just through events like "holidays around the world," and conversations about gender and ability or disability status are moved out of health class and into all disciplines.

In her essay "Curriculum as Window and Mirror," Emily Style (1996) describes the importance of making this shift and creating balance:

> Education needs to enable the student to look through window frames in order to see the realities of others and into mirrors in order to see her/his own reality reflected. Knowledge of both types of framing is basic to a balanced education which is committed to affirming the essential dialectic between the self and the world. (p. 1)

Another way to think of this is to remember that seeing and following Black leaders isn't just good for Black children; it's also good for non-Black children. Learning about trans people helps cis children expand their understanding of the world. Learning about people with disabilities—even if there are no children in the classroom with obvious disabilities—is good for children without disabilities. If not presented with an alternative view, those who have always seen themselves as "the main players on life's stage" will continue to do so (Style, 1996).

Selection of Texts and Resources

A good place to begin this effort is to include texts and other resources that curate collections of stories and perspectives that reflect the diversity of people and cultures in and out of the classroom. "When stories only reflect members of a dominant population, it reinforces ideas that sideline students of color, linguistically diverse students, single parent/multi-generation/LGBTQ+ led families, and differently-abled students" (Bryan-Gooden et al., 2019).

As Christina M. Tschida, Caitlin L. Ryan, and Anne Swenson Ticknor (2014) write in their article "Building on Windows and Mirrors: Encouraging the Disruption of 'Single Stories' Through Children's Literature,"

> The images and representations in literature (or lack of them) shape children's beliefs about who is good and who is bad, who counts and who does not, and whose experiences are deemed more important than others. (p. 30)

Their observation explains why picture books such as *Crown: An Ode to the Fresh Cut* by Derrick Barnes, *Mommy's Khimar* by Jamilah Thompkins-Bigelow, and *Julián Is a Mermaid* by Jessica Love are so powerful. Schools need to audit their classroom texts and resources to ensure that they include diverse characters and authors and that they accurately portray cultural experiences. A good resource for guiding this process is the *Culturally Responsive Curriculum Scorecard* from the Metropolitan Center for Research on Equity and the Transformation of Schools (Bryan-Gooden et al., 2019).

Diversity in texts also includes presenting new and multiple perspectives about traditional or accepted stories. Chimamanda Adichie's TED Talk "The Danger of a Single Story" brings attention to the damage to how we think about ourselves and others that results from repeatedly telling the same story about a group of people. This repeated messaging is how stereotypes develop. "The problem with stereotypes is not that they are untrue, but that they are incomplete. They make one story become the only story" (Adichie, 2009). "It is only by disrupting the single stories with narratives told from other perspectives that we form a more nuanced picture of the people, issues, or ideas at hand" (Tschida et al., 2014, p. 31).

To better illustrate the importance of telling different stories, consider the learning experience outlined in Figure 6.1, which uses the strategy of "deep viewing" as students examine the famous Will Counts photo of Elizabeth Eckford and Hazel Bryan Massery during the desegregation of Central High School in Little Rock, Arkansas, in 1957 (Finley, 2014).

This activity highlights the contributions of Elizabeth Eckford, one of the Little Rock Nine, the group of Black students who were the first to enroll in the high school. It also presents the story from a different perspective by incorporating a video clip of author David Margolick (2012) describing the relationship between Elizabeth Eckford and Hazel Bryan Massery in the years following the event. However, the activity falls short in presenting the whole story from multiple perspectives in two ways. If student discussion focuses only on the anger and actions of Hazel Bryan Massery, it will not give justice to the bravery and perseverance of Elizabeth Eckford. It is important that the teacher reframe the story by asking questions

Figure 6.1

VISUAL LEARNING EXAMPLE

1. Individually, students examine the photo and answer the question *What is your first impression about what is happening?*

2. Students divide the photo into four quadrants, study the details, and record the people, objects, and activities/actions they see in each quadrant on the chart.

Quadrant #1	Quadrant #2
People:	People:
Objects:	Objects:
Actions/Activities:	Actions/Activities:
Quadrant #3	Quadrant #4
People:	People:
Objects:	Objects:
Actions/Activities:	Actions/Activities:

3. They meet in small groups to discuss both their literal observations and their interpretations of the events. Questions to guide their discussion include the following:

   Literal observation:

   a. Who is the focus of the photo? Why do you think so?
   b. What do you think is happening? What details from the photo make you think so?
   c. Where do you think this is taking place? What details from the photo make you think so?
   d. When do you think this is happening? What details from the photo make you think so?

   Interpretation:

   a. What might the two women in the photo have in common? Why do you think so?
   b. What *don't* we know from the photo?
   c. What questions would you want to ask the photographer?
   d. What questions would you want to ask the people in the photo?

   Students participate in a whole-group discussion around the following questions:

   a. What important message do you think the photo conveys?
   b. Do you think the image is biased? Why or why not?

4. Students view and listen to the video of David Margolick discussing his book *Elizabeth and Hazel: Two Women of Little Rock* (www.youtube.com/watch?v=X46XuWzpFgA#t=106) and then discuss the following questions as a large group:

   a. What message does the narrator of the story want to convey?
   b. How does the video change your reactions to the original image, if at all?
   c. How will you approach other socially charged photos? Why?

about Elizabeth to change a single story of oppression and anger to a more complex one that includes power and hope. In addition, the resource used to further explore the story behind the picture is written by an outsider—a white male—years after the event occurred. Adding sources, such as the discussion of the events and its aftermath by Elizabeth Eckford, Terrence Roberts, and Melba Beals on the NPR podcast episode "Walking to Class, into the History Books" (Chideya, 2007), changes the narrative and offers a full accounting of the events, presenting another story. Understanding how all of these variables interact requires thoughtful analysis of texts and resources and is another example of why social-identity work by curriculum designers is so important.

Another common failure of curriculum is the elimination of stories. "The *null curriculum*... the absence of certain experiences, interactions, and discourses... can actually be immensely present in what students are learning" (Milner, 2017). This observation is particularly true when curriculum intentionally avoids important current topics and events, such as racism and other social justice issues. When educators teach using the null curriculum, they send a message that the missing stories are not important, and they are "complicit in maintaining the status quo" (Milner, 2017).

To benefit from the exploration of diverse cultures and to develop an appreciation for the uniqueness and individualism of their classmates, students will need to draw upon the social and emotional skills discussed in Chapter 4. Learning experiences that focus on self- and social awareness will provide strategies students need so they can reflect on their own identity and their place in the world.

Student Voice and Choice

Designing curriculum from an "asset mindset" is another way to honor students' cultural and experiential backgrounds and build off their strengths and interests. An *asset*, simply defined, is a useful or valuable thing or quality. Students' culture and life experiences are honored and seen as assets to learning when their experiences become part of what and how they learn.

The challenge for many teachers is that the lives of the young people in their classroom may be very different from their own. Even if teachers think their students have had similar lived experiences, they should still take the time to better understand students' strengths, interests, and lifestyles. The best way to incorporate student assets into learning is to invite students to shape what they learn, how they learn, and how they share their learning with others. In Chapter 5, I described how to create a strong framework for involving students in the process of cocreating the curriculum. Doing so allows them to be active participants in curriculum design, as illustrated in the example of students selecting their focus for examining the essential question *Is justice guaranteed?* Students' families are also assets that can be tapped by inviting them into the classroom as experts sharing their knowledge and experiences related to their cultural background (Bryan-Gooden et al., 2019; Ladson-Billings, 2014).

By opening themselves to new ideas and experiences and sharing what they learned as a result with their students, teachers create the environment for students to make choices that reflect their own identity. For example, when English teachers read and share books by authors from outside the classical canon, such as Ta-Nehisi Coates, Haruki Murakami, and Jhumpa Lahiri, or when social studies teachers help students understand the complexities of U.S. history by using texts such as *An Indigenous Peoples' History of the United States* by Roxanne Dunbar-Ortiz (2014), they model the value of listening to and learning from a diverse collection of thinkers, artists, historians, and authors.

Written Feedback

In addition to acknowledging cultural and experiential assets, teachers should recognize students' learning assets. An asset-based approach to instruction begins with acknowledging what students know and can do, rather than the more common deficit approach, which focuses on what they cannot do. This approach is particularly important for students with learning disabilities, who often receive the bulk of these negative messages. All students are capable of learning, and when they receive feedback that provides information about their strengths, needs, and next steps, as described in Chapter 4, they come to understand how to use their assets to move their learning forward. When feedback is an ongoing part of daily instruction and teachers respond to what they have learned or know about their students, students experience successes that encourage them to continue engaging in the learning process (Hammond, 2015). They develop the habits of mind and growth mindset that are foundational to learning.

Equity Criterion #2

Students have access to and are held to high expectations when they engage in tasks that strongly align to clearly articulated standards, standards are unpacked in ways they can understand and use, and they engage in feedback processes in relation to those standards.

Standards Alignment

Access to high expectations begins by ensuring that grade-level standards are used in the design of units of study and all standards are taught and assessed over the course of the year (Lalor, 2017). Designers should not modify or eliminate standards from the curriculum. Instead, a reasonable amount of standards should be prioritized in each unit, and they should be made accessible to students in ways students can use and understand. When needed, students should have the scaffolds needed to achieve them.

Learning Targets and Language Objectives

Learning targets are one way to make standards accessible to students. Learning targets present expectations for a unit using student-friendly language. In Chapter 2, I described how to embed practices into learning targets and how to use learning targets and success criteria with students. Learning targets related to content and practices are only one type that teachers should share with students. Students should also engage in lessons that address different types of thinking and social and emotional skills. The learning targets for these lessons bring students' attention to how to use these important skills to learn. In *Creating Inclusive Writing Environments in the K–12 Classroom: Reluctance, Resistance, and Strategies That Make a Difference*, Angela Stockman (2020) provides a framework for creating an inclusive workshop model and offers many different types of learning targets that teachers can use when being responsive to the learners in their classrooms. For example, some of the learning targets that she provides that address self-awareness include *I can become more self-aware by*

- Exploring how my self-perception compared to how others think of me.
- Distinguishing my intentions from my impact.
- Inviting others to illuminate my potential biases.
- Practicing how to speak the truth in ways that will be heard.
- Reflecting on my experiences as I develop self-awareness. (Stockman, 2020, p. 221)

Learning targets known as "language objectives" provide equitable access by making language expectations clear to English language learners. Language objectives articulate the academic-language functions, structures, and vocabulary that learners need so they can fully participate in a lesson and meet the grade-level standards (Himmel, 2012). Language-function objectives focus on how to use language for different purposes, such as agreeing and disagreeing, comparing, questioning, and sequencing. For example, I can use the phrases *similar to* and *different from* to compare objects. Language-structure objectives include information about voice, tenses, questioning patterns, sentence structures, adverbs, and adjectives. I can use adjectives (*amused, bored, successful*) to describe my feelings and express my voice in writing. Vocabulary language objectives bring attention to the words needed to communicate within the lesson. For example, we can use precise terms such as *solid, liquid,* and *gas* to describe states of matter.

Quality language objectives complement the knowledge and skills identified in the content objective (Himmel, 2012). Like learning targets, language objectives should be used in all content areas. For example, the mathematics learning target "I can approximate the probability of a chance event" is connected to the language objective "I can use the words *likely, not likely* to express probability." It is important to note that these language objectives are not about requiring children to speak "proper" English or penalizing those who may use an American English variation, such as African American Vernacular English or Black American Sign Language, but are used to support student understanding and participation in the lesson.

Rubrics and Checklists

Another way to ensure that students have equitable access to standards is through checklists and rubrics. As we learned in Chapter 2, all standards that have been included as desired results for the unit should also be included in the checklist or rubric. The checklist or rubric breaks down the standards and explains them in terms of the task the students will complete. Checklists define the expectations for a task, and rubrics describe the expectations at different levels.

Unfortunately, instead of providing a scaffold for learning, some rubrics reinforce the message of defeat that many students already feel. When a rubric is structured from 4, proceeding down to level 1, it communicates that the only works worth reading are those able to meet exemplary status. A rubric that begins with 1 and works up to 4 or better yet, avoids numbers all together, communicates a developmental approach to learning. When a rubric is written to describe what is evident in the student work, as shown in Figure 6.2, it can provide a scaffold for moving along the progressions of learning, and it reinforces the growth mindset necessary for learning, as described in Chapter 4.

Rubrics must also be checked for language that reinforces harmful notions related to race, gender, disability status, and class. Over time, students often learn to protect themselves from this type of negative messaging through disengagement or behavior that negates learning.

The criteria found in the rubric or checklist are important foundations to the feedback process described throughout this book. In the rubric in Figure 6.2, the criterion, *I demonstrate perseverance by completing the problem using an equation, a visual representation, and other mathematical tools,* is the basis of the classroom learning target: *I can demonstrate perseverance in solving word problems.* The feedback from the teacher to the student is based on this target:

> I am glad to see that you used an equation to solve the problem. Remember that creating a visual representation is

another way to persevere when faced with challenging problems. A visual will help you see the problem clearly, solve it accurately, and check your work.

When rubrics and checklists are used to create classroom learning targets, and learning targets and feedback are aligned to each other, they emphasize and focus students on their goal for learning and provide a pathway for getting there.

Figure 6.2

EXCERPT FROM A STRENGTHS-BASED RUBRIC

Beginning	Still Working	Got It!	Wow!
I complete the problem as quickly as possible in my head without using any mathematical tools.	I demonstrate perseverance by completing the problem using an equation.	I demonstrate perseverance by completing the problem using an equation, a visual representation, and other mathematical tools.	I demonstrate perseverance and commitment by representing and solving the problem, changing strategy when necessary, and using a different strategy to ensure the answer is correct.

Equity Criterion #3

Students engage in authentic experiences that develop relationships and build human and social capital and civic equity by using curriculum-embedded performance assessments that connect to the community and the world outside school.

Curriculum-embedded performance assessments are intentionally designed to engage students in meaningful experiences that empower them to take charge of their own learning for worthwhile purposes. When we look at curriculum-embedded performance assessments through the lens of equity, we see their capacity to develop students' human and social capital and civic equity. Curriculum-embedded performance assessments empower students to believe in themselves, take positive risks, and self-advocate to achieve their goals. When students engage in activities with their peers and with members of their community, they develop the social networks that provide support when they face challenges and build connections that may help them in the future. As students experience the benefits and impact of working for causes within their community, they set the stage to become policymakers within their own communities in the future. The following examples demonstrate the lasting impact of student engagement in meaningful and authentic work of their choosing.

Example #1. In English class, students read texts that examine personal journeys of identity. Students reflected on their own understanding of who they are and the factors that influence this understanding. Students selected the way in which to share their story and learn with others, modeled on one of the texts and modalities they studied in class. One student felt particularly empowered by this learning experience. He deeply connected with the novel *Simon vs. the Homo Sapiens Agenda* by Becky Albertalli and decided to write and perform an original song that shared his journey to understanding his identity as a gay teenager.

In this example, the student had the knowledge and skills to write and perform his original work and decided to use his talent to express a personal aspect of his own identity. His work developed from his human capital—his beliefs about himself, his talent, and his desire to share his journey to help others who might be struggling with their own identity.

Example #2. As part of the health science curriculum, students were asked to attend a school club meeting, volunteer their time, or take some other action in a community organization related to a topic studied in class. After attending the event, students reported back to the class on how the organization or event they attended addressed the issue they chose. After reading and discussing an article on food deserts in class, one student decided to volunteer at the Saturday farmers market in the school gymnasium, which was created to bring fresh fruits and vegetables to the urban community in which he lives. Although the students were only asked to attend once, this student returned often to the farmers market and developed a relationship with one of the vendors, who offered him a summer job.

In this food-desert example, we see social capital at work. When the student attended the farmers market, he met people who saw his commitment and passion for ensuring everyone had access to good food. The relationships he established with members of the organization and the vendor later led to a job. When students develop a network of relationships with different people and organizations, they are building social capital that will help them to achieve their goals. As seen in both examples, human and social capital that is built through "meaningful contact with peers and educators can create new possibilities" (Smith et al., 2017).

Example #3. In a middle school social studies classroom, students read about the arrival of Europeans in America and examined the perspectives of Christopher Columbus, Queen Isabelle and King Ferdinand of Spain, and the Taino, the Indigenous people living in the Caribbean at the time. The students then investigated diverse opinions about the celebration of Columbus Day within their community, where many of the students live on the Native American reservation. After their investigation, a group of students petitioned the local town board to change the Columbus Day Parade to the Indigenous People's Day Parade.

These students, some with connections to Indigenous nations and people, advocated for a change that was deeply personal to their culture and community. By learning how to respond to a civic matter in a way that produces change in policy, these students are preparing for civic participation later in life. Civic equality develops when people are equipped to take action to change policies and practices that affect them and their neighborhoods (Rogers, 2019).

Curriculum-embedded performance assessments that lead to such results as those just described call for deep thinking (discussed in Chapter 3). Students analyze and evaluate the world around them to determine where to focus their attention and how to best use their skills. In this way they cultivate their talents, develop relationships, and work within their communities on their own terms. As students develop a critical consciousness of the world around them and respond to an invitation to make what they value part of the curriculum, their actions can address many social justice issues. They may propose creating a Peanut Butter and Jelly Club to support a local homeless shelter, acting as translators for newcomers and their families, or reviewing school and district dress codes for racial or gender bias. Once students realize they are trusted by their teachers to recognize how they can change the world, they can—and do—find all sorts of opportunities, big and small, to do so. A useful resource for teachers looking to support this worldview for their students is the Teaching Tolerance Social Justice Standards and related materials, available at www.tolerance.org/frameworks/social-justice-standards.

Educators who truly believe in the potential of curriculum-embedded performance assessment to develop human and social capital and civic equity must support the decision of their students as to where and how the students will carry out their learning. Again, it's critical that curriculum designers examine their personal biases in this regard. Educators need to explore what might be preventing them from fully supporting students in pursuing social justice issues, and teachers who want to do so should not have to do it alone. Administrators must support teachers in providing these types of learning experiences for their students. Administrators may be called upon to educate the school board members and parents as to the benefits of allowing students to determine how they work in their communities.

Equity Criterion #4

Students engage in their learning through activities that are meaningful and contextualized and call for their active participation in the process.

Too often students spend their time in class listening to teachers talk, completing worksheets, or answering low-level questions. As a result, some students have become complacent, others use distracting behaviors, and still others simply leave the educational system. The three activities described in the following sections—collaboration, discussion and oral language, and cognitive routines—have been proven to have a strong positive effect on student learning by actively engaging students and drawing upon the culture and experiences of many of them.

Collaboration

Collaboration, or cooperative learning, is a powerful instructional approach, especially for learning concepts, verbal problem solving, categorizing, spatial problem solving, retention and memory, and guessing-judging-predicting (Hattie, 2012). It reflects the collectivist archetype of many cultures. Hammond (2015) describes this archetype and compares it with the individualistic model as follows:

> Collectivist societies emphasize relationships, interdependence within a community, and cooperative learning. Individualistic societies emphasize individual achievement and independence. In America, the dominant culture is individualistic, while the cultures of many African American, Latino, Pacific Islander, and Native American communities lean more toward collectivism. (p. 25)

The value of individualism is very evident in classrooms throughout the United States. Students often sit in rows, completing worksheets independently. Teachers often prefer silence to noise, and students enjoy competitive learning games as well as competing against each other for grades, awards, and recognition. A classroom where this is the norm is not welcoming to a student who comes from a collectivist culture where decisions are made based on the needs of the group, where the common good is the impetus behind individual work, and where individual achievements are seen as success for all.

Experiences involving design thinking and creative thinking (explained in Chapter 3) need to become routine practices, allowing students to work collaboratively to solve problems. When students are presented with or uncover problems within the context of their own community, they can draw upon their own lived experiences to ideate or brainstorm possible solutions. For example, when I was working with the students from MS 45 in the Bronx (see Chapter 4) to examine what could be done in their community to address the pollution problem, one student explained how her grandmother cooked rice in plastic bags (a process that I came to learn is called *sous vide*). The other students in the group connected to this shared experience and decided that creating reminders of common uses for plastic bags was a good way to engage members of their community in recycling.

Discussion and Oral Language

Discussion is a way for students to process and make sense of new information and ideas. When students talk, they are thinking. Yet, according to many research studies, teachers are still doing most of the talking in the classroom (Hattie, 2012). In Chapter 5, we examined civic discourse. The strategies shared there—generating quality questions, using protocols, creating criteria, and reflecting on the process—are mainstays of quality discussion and should be used to guide classroom discussion. These strategies allow all students' voices to be heard, so everyone benefits from the conversation. Discussion is also a proven strategy for English language learners because it provides them with the practice necessary for oral language development (Baker et al., 2014; ELSF, n.d.). To make discussion most productive, students benefit from the following:

- A common experience, such as viewing videos, images, demonstrations, models, or reading shared texts, which builds background knowledge and helps students support each other in developing the language for sharing their thinking (Baker et al., 2014)
- A wide range of talking experiences, beginning with partner or small-group discussions before progressing to large or whole-group exchanges
- Protocols, such as those shared in Chapter 5, but also supports such as think-pair-share and accountable talk stems—prompts that guide students in productive conversations

Research also suggests that English language learners benefit from discussions in their native language. Speaking in one's native language honors students' cultural background, develops their native language skills, and allows them to think at high levels without having to worry about their level of English proficiency (Lander, 2019/2020). Many states have recognized the value of multilingualism by awarding a "seal of biliteracy" to students for achievement in two languages upon graduation (Lander, 2019/2020). An equitable education provides students with the opportunity to develop their native speaking skills along with English proficiency.

Directly related to discussion is the use of oral language. Incorporating opportunities for oral language is a cultural approach to learning, as described by Hammond (2015):

> Some cultures have relied heavily on the spoken word rather than the written word to convey, preserve, and reproduce knowledge from generation to generation. By telling stories and coding knowledge into songs, chants, proverbs, and poetry, groups with a strong oral tradition record and sustain their cultures and cultural identities by word of mouth. (p. 28)

For example, in Chapter 4 we examined role-playing different characters as a means for developing empathy and appreciation of different perspectives. Role-playing is a form of storytelling and includes having students retell stories, develop innovative versions of stories, or create their own original stories. Storytelling and discussion are effective instructional strategies when oral language plays a prominent role in students' everyday lives.

Cognitive Routines

Cognitive routines support equity by providing students with independent learning strategies that are effective in addressing different types of thinking. Cognitive routines are mental maneuvers learners can use to process information. Typically, scaffolds such as graphic organizers, written outlines, or fill-in-the-blank charts are under the control of the teacher. The teacher decides when they will be used and how. When students are taught cognitive routines, they know why, when, and how to use these self-generated tools. This understanding allows students more control over their own learning. Cognitive routines are beneficial to all students because they free up space in the brain for students to think about *what* they are learning rather than *how* they are learning it. For English language learners, cognitive routines can help make "content comprehensible and serve as a source for related writing and speaking activities" (Baker et al., 2014). Three strategies for establishing cognitive routines with students are learning targets and success criteria, acronyms, and self-questioning strategies.

Learning targets and success criteria. In Chapter 2, we examined the value of sharing learning targets and success criteria with students, and how students can use them to monitor their learning. The repeated use of the same learning target and success criteria provides students with a cognitive routine. For example, repeated use of the following steps will establish them as a routine for students to use to make inference:

> I can make an inference about the text by
> - Stating what the text says.
> - Thinking about what I know.
> - Making a connection between the two.

Acronyms. Acronyms are similar to success criteria. The major difference is that the first letter of each step of the process creates a word that a student can easily remember. For example, students annotate primary sources using the acronym SOAP: **S**ource, **O**ccasion, **A**udience, **P**urpose. The acronym identifies what students need to look for within a document but not how to look for it. Without knowing how to find the information in the document that reveals the source, occasion, audience, and purpose, the acronym serves no purpose. Students need to know how to look for information—such as the date, author, events described, locations mentioned, vocabulary, and voice—that indicates when, why, and for whom the document was written. The acronym only works as a cognitive routine when it triggers the actions the students must take for achieving their goal.

Self-questioning strategies. These strategies provide students with a series of questions for approaching a task. For example, students may use the following three questions for analyzing images:

- What do I notice?
- What do I see that makes me say that?
- What more can I find out?

These three questions prompt students to examine what is evident in an image, what conclusions they draw as a result, and what additional information they need so they can accurately interpret the event depicted in the image (*New York Times*, n.d.).

Sharing a strategy with students is not enough for it to be considered a cognitive routine, nor is it advisable to share too many of these strategies. For the tool or strategy to become routine, the teacher needs to repeatedly model how to use it and then the students must practice using it. When students have internalized the routine, they can independently apply it when needed. Sharing too many routines with students can actually interfere with their use. It's best to share those cognitive routines that can be used across disciplines, texts, and modalities and are useful outside the classroom. The cognitive routines just described are useful to students because they meet these criteria and help build their media toolbox (as discussed in Chapter 5).

Equity Criterion #5

Students become independent and self-regulated learners by setting and monitoring goals and reflecting on their learning.

Self-regulated learners are aware of the strategies they can use to learn; they understand when, how, and why these strategies operate; they set goals and monitor their own performance; and they attribute outcomes to factors within their control (Resnick & Hall, 2003; Zimmerman, 2000). Self-regulation begins with students' belief that they can learn. Students are taught about growth mindset and habits of mind (see Chapter 4) and develop self-questioning tools and prompts to support their own favorable beliefs about their learning (Hammond, 2015; Smith et al., 2017). When students believe they can learn, they are more open and willing to engage in learning and the goal setting and reflective practices described in the remainder of this section (Hammond, 2015; Smith et al., 2017).

Teachers support their students when they believe their students are capable learners and make it clear to students that they believe all students can and will learn. Without these elements, teachers may share strategies so students can engage in goal setting and reflection, but their actions outside the focused lesson may indicate otherwise. Teachers may fall back into the previous habit of structuring the learning so much that students do not have the opportunity to use their metacognitive skill in new and unknown situations where it counts the most. The teachers' job in these cases is to coach students through the process of setting and achieving goals.

Setting and Achieving Goals

Setting and achieving goals is a multistep process that involves knowing how to write a goal and having a plan of action for achieving the goal that includes strategies for overcoming challenges. A good way to teach students how to write a goal is by having them examine and critique models. Students need to understand how to set clear and concise goals that require an appropriate degree of productive struggle. The goal cannot be so easily attainable that it does not require conscientious effort or so difficult that it seems unattainable.

With a clear understanding of what a goal is, students can set their own. Students' goals should be guided by task criteria that have been shared through rubrics, checklists, or learning targets with success criteria. Criteria can be generated by the teacher, but they are most powerful when students create them using language that reflects their cultural learning style (Hammond, 2015). When students work with criteria by examining models and exemplars, conferencing with teachers, and engaging in peer-feedback sessions, they are equipped to use the criteria to establish and monitor their own goals, as shown in this example:

> Students work with a checklist to guide the writing process. They use the checklist to examine their work and set a goal for their writing. Students write their goal on an index card, which they place in a pocket chart that hangs in the classroom. They conference with the teacher on what they can do to meet their writing goal and then continue to work on their writing. At the end of each writing workshop, the teacher invites students who have met their goal to share their work with the class and what they did to meet their goal.

Once a goal is in place, students must have strategies and recognize when and know how to seek out resources for meeting their goal. The most difficult part of goal work is the monitoring and adjustment process. Often students understand what they need to work on but do not have the tools or strategies to do so. As shown in the following example, making challenges and strategies transparent is beneficial to everyone:

> Students keep a learning log as they work on their projects. At the end of each work session, the teacher asks students to reflect on the following questions: *What was easy for you today? Why? What did you find was challenging? What strategy or resource did you use to persevere?* Every few days the teacher asks the students to share a success and a strategy that led to the success, or a problem or obstacle and what they did to overcome it. The teacher records strategies and their purposes on a class chart as a reference for future work sessions.

The reflection and sharing process helps students monitor their progress and share their accomplishments. All goals, big and small, need to be celebrated. Celebrating the goal acknowledges the small successes that build learning.

Metacognition

Simply defined, metacognition is thinking about thinking. It includes being aware that there are different ways to think, understanding that there are strategies for addressing different types of thinking, and then applying those understandings to one's thinking (Anderson & Krathwohl, 2001). To become self-regulated learners, students need to be aware of when meaning making works, as well as when it breaks down; when they find learning easy and when they find it difficult; when the strategy they are using is successful, as well as when it isn't. Most important, students need to take what works for them as a learner and apply it when learning is a challenge. For any of this to happen, they need to be aware of their own thinking.

Students can learn to be metacognitive when they are prompted to reflect on their learning (Smith et al., 2017). Questions, such as those shared in the goal-setting lesson described earlier, prompt students to think about their thinking: *What was easy for you today? Why? What did you find challenging? What strategy or resource did you use to persevere?* (See Chapter 4 for additional questions and prompts to support metacognition.) When students develop metacognition as a habit of mind, they have the key piece in becoming independent, self-regulated learners.

Summing Up

Curriculum that attends to equity begins with examining one's identity and place in the world to ensure the curriculum does not unintentionally incorporate the biases of its creators. Curriculum and classroom practices that build equity honor the cultural and experiential backgrounds of students, provide access to high expectations and learning experiences, develop students' human and social capital and civic equity, engage students in meaningful learning experiences, and provide strategies that students can use to become self-regulated, independent learners. For curriculum to achieve these goals, students must be active participants in creating their own learning experiences.

 CHAPTER REFLECTION

Use the following chart to help you reflect on how your school or classroom incorporates the tools, strategies, or practices shared throughout the chapter.

Equity: Addressing the individualized attributes of students (culture, race, gender, ability, language) so they can engage in their learning and eliminating those practices that prevent students from reaching their full potential.

Curriculum Reflection Questions:

1. Have those who are involved in the curriculum design process examined their own identity to ensure they do not unintentionally carry biases into the curriculum?
2. To what degree do books, images, and other resources represent a wide range of cultures and identities, providing both windows and mirrors?
3. Does the curriculum disrupt single-story representations of people and events?
4. Does the unit explicitly communicate valued outcomes related to practices, deep thinking, social and emotional learning, and civic participation and discourse?
5. Does the curriculum ensure that all courses and classrooms at the same level are aligned to standards?
6. Do the curriculum-embedded performance assessments engage students with authentic audiences and purposes? Do these experiences build human and social capital and encourage students to work to develop civic equity in their community?

Strengths, Needs, and Possible Next Steps

Instruction Reflection Questions:

1. Are students made aware of standards in a way they can understand and use? Do teachers
   - Share learning targets and language objectives with students?
   - Use standards to design checklists and rubrics?
   - Use criteria to provide students with feedback or engage students in peer or self-feedback?

2. Are students made aware of their assets and encouraged to use them in learning? Does feedback provided include strengths, needs, and next steps?

3. What type of high-impact, active-learning strategies are students encouraged to use? Do students have opportunities to work cooperatively, participate in discussions, and use cognitive routines?

4. Do students have the opportunity to set and monitor goals? Are they taught strategies for doing so? Are their accomplished goals celebrated?

5. Do students engage in metacognition? What questions, prompts, or strategies do teachers use to support students' metacognition?

Strengths, Needs, and Possible Next Steps

7

Putting It All Together

This book began with an exploration of how schools can start designing a curriculum that matters by examining their mission and vision statements. For the Southampton School District in New York, discussed in Chapter 1, review of its vision and mission led to the articulation of criteria to guide the development of the curriculum and a professional development and design project. Teachers from every discipline and every grade level participated in this multiyear initiative. As they deepened their understanding of a quality curriculum, they grew in their understanding of each of the elements—practices, deep thinking, social and emotional learning, civic engagement and civic discourse, and equity—and how they could begin to implement the elements in the classroom. Although they still have work to do, evidence of the initiative's influence, including teacher and student feedback, observations of teachers' practice, and the examination of student work, all indicate a positive impact on student learning.

In Oak Park Elementary School District 97 in Illinois, Superintendent Carol Kelley worked with district and community members to develop a shared vision: to create a positive learning environment for all students that is equitable, inclusive, and focused on the whole child. The curriculum committee was made up of teachers and coaches, including Renita S. Banks, Ruth Barker, Jennifer Browning, Jennifer Cofsky, Nancy Hoehne, Mary Kelly, Jennifer Logan, Kiera Moody, Veena Rajashekar, Hannah Tatro, David Wawzenek, and

Mohogany Williams. They were led by Tawanda Lawrence, senior director of curriculum, instruction, and assessment; and Elizabeth Parkinson, curriculum specialist grades K–5.

The committee was charged with updating an existing written curriculum that had been created during a previous design project. The committee's first step was to identify criteria, as described in Chapter 1, that would guide the revision process and ensure the curriculum's alignment to the district's vision. The review process revealed the strengths of the existing curriculum as well as steps that could be taken to improve it. The curriculum-design team learned that their curriculum strongly aligned to the standards. The review also revealed the need to design curriculum-embedded performance assessments to provide students with meaningful experiences to engage with authentic audiences and purposes. This became the focus of the work for the curriculum-design team.

At PS 108, the Philip J. Abinanti School in the Bronx, New York, Principal Charles Sperrazza and Assistant Principals Lori Solano and Georgette Valente wanted the curriculum to promote their school's vision of an equitable education for all students. They invited me to do a focused review of their curriculum, using the criteria described in Chapter 6. The review revealed that the curriculum provided access to standards through a variety of methods, including learning targets and guiding questions. It was also evident that teachers engaged students through a variety of instructional strategies, including some thinking routines, and used formative assessments to monitor student learning. With a strong foundation and a school culture that fostered professional learning, the school was positioned to begin the revision process.

The PS 108 Instructional Leadership Team was charged with this task. Teachers on the team included Laura Bennett, Kelly Bergin, Dominque Breitenbach, Kristin Cerbone, Patricia Forrest, Denise Hefter, Laura Loughran McAuliffe, Rosa Mancini, Courtney O'Grady, Selina Olivo, Janine Paparelli, Jessica Polgano, and LuAnne Riley. The committee's work began with unpacking the criteria for an equitable curriculum and discussing how each criterion affects student learning. Based on this common understanding of what makes a quality curriculum and the review of the existing curriculum, the team decided to focus their attention on the following: (1) creating language objectives to complement learning targets, (2) identifying specific social and emotional competencies and related learning activities for each unit of study, and (3) developing curriculum-embedded performance assessments that engaged students with the local community. As the teachers worked to refine their curriculum, they also deepened their understanding of how strategic implementation could affect student learning.

Although Southampton, Oak Park District 97, and PS 108 each entered the design of a curriculum that matters in different ways, they all had the same goal: they wanted a curriculum aligned to their vision of an excellent and equitable education for all students. These schools recognized that curriculum, as the tool that teachers use to make instructional decisions, could be a powerful vehicle in achieving that goal. When curriculum aligns to what is valued, it sends a message that teachers should spend time in class working to address important academic, intellectual, and social and emotional learning goals.

As an educator who has worked with hundreds of schools, I have come to see curriculum as an entry point into critical discussions about practice. When teachers are given the time to think about what they teach, why they teach it, and who they teach, they are better able to make the strategic decisions necessary to engage all students in their learning—the ultimate goal of this book. When teachers engage in professional learning centered around the elements of a curriculum that matters, they develop a deeper understanding of each and can leverage the overlap to build equitable learning experiences for all students.

Throughout this book I have invited you to work with the following chart. This chart was designed as a tool for thinking about how each element is addressed in your school and how it translates or could translate into your curriculum. If an element exists, it needs to be identified using familiar terms and then strategically incorporated into the curriculum and implemented in the classroom. Recognizing how your school addresses the elements is important because it identifies the foundation that already exists.

REFLECTION CHART FOR ELEMENTS OF A CURRICULUM THAT MATTERS

Practices: The applications of an idea, a belief, or a method to construct understanding; often associated with specific disciplines but frequently found to be applicable across disciplines.

Strengths, Needs, and Possible Next Steps

Deep Thinking: Thinking that allows for application, extension, and creation of new ideas rather than a general understanding of content, knowledge, and ideas.

Strengths, Needs, and Possible Next Steps

Social and Emotional Learning: Learning that includes developing an understanding of one's self to achieve personal goals, understand and appreciate others, self-regulate, develop relationships, and make good decisions.

Strengths, Needs, and Possible Next Steps

Civic Engagement: Active participation as a local, state, national, or global community member. **Civic Discourse:** Successful participation in conversations with those who do not hold the same view or opinion and to learn from the experience.

Strengths, Needs, and Possible Next Steps

Equity: Addressing the individualized attributes of students (e.g., culture, race, gender, ability, language) so they can engage in their learning, and eliminating those practices that prevent students from reaching their full potential.

Strengths, Needs, and Possible Next Steps

Recording your connections to the elements also helps you determine what you are not doing well and areas you need to explore further. Areas in need of further development provide you with an entry point into the creation of a curriculum that matters, leading you to further investigate the element and integrate new ideas and strategies into the curriculum and classroom instruction.

Designing a curriculum that matters requires changing the lens for viewing the curriculum so you can clearly recognize each individual element separately and how you can use it to support student learning, as illustrated in the example in Appendix A. Only when you recognize how each element is evidenced in the curriculum can it be purposefully integrated into classroom instruction. Ensuring the curriculum attends to practices, deep thinking, social and emotional learning, and civic engagement and discourse provides a strong foundation for building equity through curriculum. However, the hard work of examining one's own identity and place in the world is a necessary prerequisite to leveraging the other elements to build equity. The curriculum must be reviewed to ensure it does not unintentionally carry the biases of those involved in its creation or review.

In closing, I want to give you one last tool for incorporating the framework of a curriculum that matters into your practice. Although this book is organized using the five elements, it addresses the elements through the attributes of a high-quality curriculum discussed in an earlier book: organizing centers, standards alignment and placement, diversified assessment system, curriculum-embedded performance assessment, and learning activities (Lalor, 2017). The checklist in Appendix B is helpful in determining how these attributes are used to address each element of the framework for a curriculum that matters.

Designing a curriculum that matters is a journey. It requires a deep examination of one's self, an openness to new ideas and instructional approaches, and a willingness to grow and change established and rooted practices. Although teachers can take steps to incorporate strategies in their classrooms, they alone cannot achieve the desired impact that results in an equitable learning environment for all students. The practices within the school must support this effort, with the school leadership leading the way.

If we want students to pursue their own pathway in life that is built off their interests and talents, classrooms must be places where students engage in learning as practitioners in the field examining issues that are meaningful and relevant to their own lives. Schools must support the transdisciplinary nature of this work by allowing flexibility in content and scheduling for students to work together with teacher mentors.

If we want students to think deeply and develop a critical consciousness of the world around them, classrooms must be places where students engage in inquiry around current events that matter to them, apply their learning in new and unfamiliar ways, and address problems that may not always end with resolution. Schools must focus on the process of learning rather than having the right answer and educate parents and other stakeholders on the complexity of supporting deep thinking in the classroom.

If we want students to deepen their understanding of themselves and others, they must regularly engage in reflection. If we want students to develop strong relationships with each other, classrooms much be places where students work collaboratively. Schools must demonstrate the value of these skills by protecting time daily for students to engage in learning activities that develop their social and emotional well-being.

If we want students to be active members of their communities, classrooms must be places where students interact with the community. Schools must work with community businesses and parents to foster partnerships. Boards of Education must invite students to share their opinion on issues, as well as serve as an authentic audience for student work.

If we want students to become independent and self-regulated learners, classrooms must be places where students manage projects, engage in productive struggle, and feel comfortable seeking assistance. Classrooms must develop routine structures that help students develop as assessment-capable learners who are able to explain what they are learning, how they are doing, and what they should do next. Schools must show more concern with learning than the grade book and focus on finding meaningful ways to monitor student learning and share that information with parents and other stakeholders.

If we want students to become healthy and happy individuals, classrooms must be places where students are heard, their identity and individuality are valued, and they are under the care of educators who open their minds and hearts to their students.

The written curriculum is a starting place to build equity because it concretizes the stated values and beliefs of schools' missions and visions into actionable steps for teachers. The process of examining and designing the curriculum through the lenses discussed in this book can be the catalyst for classroom implementation that create the equitable learning spaces we so desire. It takes time and patience to examine, revise, and create a curriculum that incorporates the elements of a curriculum that matters. It takes bold action to implement it. The result is worth the effort—because the impact on student learning is worth the effort.

Acknowledgments

If you take a look around my house, mixed in with the historical arti-facts, the pictures that pay homage to my ancestral home in Italy, and the photos of my children at various stages of their lives are fly-ing pigs. I first became enamored with flying pigs after reading David Weisner's *Tuesday*. When I found an actual wooden figure of a fly-ing pig, I began to seek them out and scatter them around my house. These seemingly misplaced items serve as a reminder, not only to me and my family but anyone entering my home, that anything is possible.

That message has been a mantra throughout my whole life, taught to me by immigrant grandparents who came here to make a better life for themselves and their families, and my parents, Jessie and Mike Di Michele, who provided me with support to achieve my goals. It is a message that I have tried to pass down to my children. I have been rewarded in seeing how they work hard to achieve their goals and establish their place in life; William as he pursues his degree as a physician assistant, Catherine as she works as a cardiac-thoracic ICU nurse, and Joseph as he begins college as an English major.

My belief that anything is possible was tested during the long months of March, April, and May 2020, when I watched Cather-ine come and go from North Shore University Hospital, caring for COVID-19 patients. She and her fellow nurses, the doctors, and staff in the cardiac-thoracic ICU were pushed to their limits. While they were used to taking caring of critically ill patients, never so many at one time, and with so much uncertainty. Yet they did it and once again proved anything is possible. They, and others like them, have my appreciation and admiration.

"Anything is possible" is also the basis for this book. Creating a curriculum that matters takes time. It is a process that involves deep reflection and change. But it is possible... and necessary so that all students can live their lives fully.

In writing this book, I have many people to thank. I would not have been able to complete it without their support. I want to first thank ASCD editor Genny Ostertag, who believed in the message of this book and worked with me so it was framed in a way educators could practically implement these valued priorities in the classroom.

I am particularly grateful for the schools and educators I have seen work to provide the best possible learning environments for their students, particularly those whose stories I share in this book. The majority of my time in education has been as an educational consultant. To grow in my own practice, I rely on the willingness of others to think through different ideas, try new strategies, and give me feedback. All of these educators have been willing to do these things for me and, as a result, have allowed me to write this book. I especially thank those educators who welcomed me as colleague and friend, including Larrilee Jemiola, Virginia McGovern, Kim Milton, Nancy Wicker, Julio Delgado, John Wendt, Lori Ferraro, and Charles Sperrazzo. I particularly want to thank Charles for taking time out of his busy schedule to provide me with thoughtful feedback, especially when the writing wasn't easy.

I am grateful to the women of Learner-Centered Initiatives: Giselle Martin-Kniep, Joanne Picone-Zocchia, Diane Cunningham, Jennifer Borgioli Binis, Liz Locatelli, Jonelle Rocke, Reshma Ramkellawan-Arteaga, Marianne Mueller, and Patti Miller. We have spent years learning together, and I am a better person and consultant because of it. I miss our meetings and adventures. I thank Giselle for starting me on this path and, along with Joanne, supporting me on my journey.

Thank you to Diane for her ongoing friendship and for giving me feedback throughout the writing process, and a special thank you to

Liz who helped me to form my ideas into words. A big thank you to Jenn for her feedback and advice particularly on the equity chapter. I also want to thank Diana Fiege, who was willing to share her experiences with service learning. Our conversations helped shape my thinking about civic engagement and equity. Thank you also to Kerin Cunningham, whose illustration I share at the beginning of the acknowledgments—may you all be inspired by her version of the flying pig!

I am very lucky to be surrounded by friends and family who I can always rely on. I greatly appreciate the many years of friendship from Kathleen Wallace, and whose daughter, my goddaughter, Paige Wallace, works tirelessly to be the best hockey player she can be and embodies "anything is possible" in the way she lives her 14-year-old life. My dear friends Pamela Slack Damboise, Ann Chauvin, Stephanie Forman, and Kristen Usaitis: I looked forward every week to our Zoom calls and can't wait until we are all able to gather together again.

I dedicate this book to my family—all of them—my husband and children, my first family, and my extended family. I am very lucky to have them as a constant presence in my life. I am thankful that my brother Michael Di Michele, my sister-in-law Lisa, and my nephews and niece Michael, Matthew, and Maddalyn have managed family vacations all these years. I appreciate family holidays with my sister- and brother-in-law Ann and Paul Pearson and my nephew and niece Eric and Sara. My extended family, who despite distance and busy lives, manage to be a solid foundation for me and for each other: my Aunt Rose, who we miss, Uncle Joe, Joseph, Kate, Rich, Ludmila, Julianne, Larry, and their children; Uncle Al, Aunt Jeannie, Robert, Cynthia, Lisa, Anthony, and their children; and Lou, JoEllen, Daniel, Julia, and Thomas.

My mother continues to be an inspiration to me. She has always believed that if you work hard enough you can do anything and has said it to my children over and over again, and now they believe it too.

Most of all, thank you to my husband Bill and our children, William, Catherine, and Joseph, who have learned that my constant praise, excitement, questions, reminders, and speeches are expressions of love—I only want what is best for you. I hope that one day, you, too, will tell your children, anything is possible.

Appendix A: Unit

The abbreviated unit shown in Figure A.1 incorporates the elements of a curriculum that matters: practices, deep thinking, social and emotional learning, civic engagement and discourse, and equity. Before reading the explanation that follows, see what evidence you can find of each element.

Figure A.1

RIGHTS AND OPPORTUNITIES UNIT

Unit Title: Rights and Opportunities	
Essential Question: *Do we all have access to the same rights and opportunities?*	**Big Idea:** Students understand that *all people have the same rights in theory, but in practice, some people's ability to access the rights that are enjoyed by others is limited.*

Guiding Questions:

- What lessons did American society learn from the fight to address inequality during the civil rights movement of the 1960s?
- What are the responsibilities of citizens of the United States?
- When is it necessary to take social action?
- How can our ability to empathize lead to social action?

Standards *(abbreviated list)*:

Social Studies: 8.9a The civil rights movement began in the postwar era in response to long-standing inequalities in American society, and eventually brought about equality under the law, but slower progress on economic improvements. (NYSED, 2017b)

F. Civic Responsibility Practices:

6. Identify situations in which social actions are required and determine an appropriate course of action.

8. Fulfill social and political responsibilities associated with citizenship in a democratic society. (NYSED, 2017b)

2. Social awareness: Students empathize with and take the perspectives of diverse others. They understand social and ethical norms and recognize their network of supports.

A: Recognize the feelings and perspectives of others.

C: Use communication and social skills to interact effectively with others. (NYSED, 2018)

Assessment Opportunities	
Assessment Moment	Feedback Opportunity
Diagnostic: Students respond to the essential question *Do we all have access to the same rights and opportunities?* Students revisit their responses and add to or modify them as they progress through the unit.	The teacher reviews student responses to examine how students define rights and opportunities, the types of examples they use, and how they position themselves in the discussion. The teacher uses this information to determine the starting point for future discussions and the examples to use in class. The teacher reviews responses as students revise them to adjust lessons.

(*continued*)

Figure A.1 (*continued*)

RIGHTS AND OPPORTUNITIES UNIT

Assessment Opportunities—(*continued*)	
Assessment Moment	Feedback Opportunity
Formative Assessment: Students conduct and share research defining educational equity and identify key court cases and policies that have improved equitable access in education for all students over time in the United States. (8.9a)	Students conduct research individually before they meet in groups to share information. Students gather additional information to clarify and add to their research based on their discussions.
Formative Assessment: Students work in groups to create and administer a survey to identify the way in which the school and community offer equitable access to education and ways in which it can be improved. (2.A)	The teacher meets with each group to provide feedback on survey questions.
Formative Assessment: Students create a plan of action addressing an issue of their choice related to equitable education. (F.6)	Students self-assess their plan using the checklist created by the class after reviewing sample plans provided by the teacher. Students revise their plans and submit them to the teacher for written feedback. The teacher identifies examples and resources for classroom lessons based on the issues identified by the students.
Curriculum-Embedded Performance Assessment: Students apply their own definition of equitable education and evaluate its presence in their school. Students identify ways to ensure better access and opportunities (recommendations for additional arts, additional pathways for participating in the STEAM program, the addition of a humanities research program, opportunity to pursue a "seal of biliteracy," improved technology or Wi-Fi access) and present their recommendation to an appropriate audience (principal, school board, program directors, parent advisory board, school-business partners) (F.6, F.8, 2.C)	
Learning Experiences (*abbreviated list*)	

- (Standards) are explicitly identified to show alignment.
- **Bold print** illustrates what students will do.
- *Italicized print* explains why; it should align with the learning target.
- Underlined text identifies the formative assessment moments in each learning activity.

Learning Experiences *(abbreviated list)—(continued)*		
Learning Target	**Language Objective**	**Learning Activity**
I can explain the role of different leaders, individuals, and groups in the events of the civil rights movement. (8.9a)	I can identify words, phrases, and sentences that describe the most important idea in texts and videos.	Students... • **Use the Word, Phrase, Sentence Protocol to <u>read, view, and discuss</u>** *the role of different leaders, individuals, and groups* present in texts and videos about *the civil rights movement* (Project Zero, 2019).
I can analyze primary sources to determine the perspective of the author. (2.A)	I can find information in a primary source document to determine the • **S**ource, • **O**ccasion, • **A**udience, • **P**urpose.	Students... • **<u>Annotate</u> primary sources using SOAP** (**S**ource, **O**ccasion, **A**udience, **P**urpose) to *determine the different perspectives and tactics of civil rights leaders in fighting injustices.*
I can engage in quality discussion to learn. (2.C)	I can follow classroom norms for having a respectful discussion with my classmates.	Students... • **<u>Create criteria</u>** to *guide their small-group discussions.* • **Participate in <u>fish-bowl discussions</u>** in response to the guiding question "When is it necessary to take social action?" to *test out their criteria and refine it* based on what they notice. • **Provide each other with <u>feed-back</u>** based on the criteria so *group discussions are productive learning experiences.* • **<u>Create and use questions</u>** to *draw out responses and ideas from peers* during small-group and whole-class discussions to ensure all students participate.
I can examine the decisions made by individuals during the civil rights movement and their impact on overcoming injustices. (8.9a, 2.A)	I can use accountable talk stems to participate in a discussion.	Students... • **Read primary and secondary sources** on the *role of Rosa Park in the Montgomery bus boycott* to **prepare for and participate in a <u>text-based discussion</u>** using accountable talk stems around the question "Was Rosa Parks really just tired?" (Tschida et al., 2014).

(continued)

Figure A.1 (*continued*)

RIGHTS AND OPPORTUNITIES UNIT

Learning Experiences *(abbreviated list)—(continued)*		
Learning Target	**Language Objective**	**Learning Activity**

I can analyze images to draw conclusions and determine what additional information I need to accurately interpret images from the civil rights movement and today. (8.9a, F.6)	I can use questions to analyze images:
	• What do I notice?
	• What do I see that makes me say that?
	• What more can I find out?
		Students...
		• **Use questions to guide and record** their *interpretation and understanding of images from the civil rights movement and today* (*New York Times*, n.d.).
		  – What do I notice?
		  – What do I see that makes me say that?
		  – What more can I find out?
		• **Work in small groups to conduct** <u>**research**</u> to *clarify their understanding of the event illustrated in the image.*

I can analyze primary sources to identify and explain the reasons the author uses to support his claim. (2.A)	I can use text symbols to annotate text: * this is important ? I have a question • I need more information	Students... • <u>**Annotate**</u> **primary sources** to *determine the author's message.* • **Use their annotations to write a** <u>**group summary**</u> *explaining why some people opposed the aims of the civil rights movement.*
I can identify bias in a text and explain why it exists. (2.A)	I can identify adverbs that reveal the author's bias.	Students... • **Examine a list of different kinds of bias.** • <u>**Underline words**</u> that *reveal the author's bias and identify the type of bias found in the primary source.* • <u>**Research**</u> the writer and event described in the primary source to determine the *accuracy of their interpretation of the author's bias and how the author's role and situation influenced his perspective*; <u>**write and share**</u> their finding with the class.
I can evaluate educational equity from social, economic, and psychological perspectives.	I can evaluate an author's perspective by identifying his claim, reason, and evidence.	Students... • **Read a variety of texts, view videos, and examine statistics** to *analyze educational equity from social, economic, and psychological perspectives.* For each source, **students identify the claim made by the author and the reasons used to support his claim,** using the <u>claims, reasoning evidence protocol.</u>

Learning Experiences *(abbreviated list)—(continued)*		
Learning Target	Language Objective	Learning Activity
I can set a goal for my learning.	I can explain the relationship between my goal and my actions.	Students... • **Examine the work** they have completed for examining different texts: SOAP strategy, text symbols, and claims, reasoning evidence protocol. • **Reflect** on *what was easy about using each strategy and what was difficult.* • **Discuss** *strategies for addressing difficulties in small groups with other students.* • **Set a goal and identify actions** for improvement using ideas shared in groups.
I can evaluate situations to determine if social action is required. (F.6)	I can write questions to find out information.	Students... • **Research and create a definition** of equitable education. They use their definition to **survey fellow students** to *determine ways in which the school has met the criterion for equitable education and areas that could be improved.*
I can empathize with challenges faced by others to brainstorm ideas for addressing a social issue in my school. (2.A)	I can use the words *problem* and *solution* when sharing my ideas.	• **Participate in a brainstorming session** to *identify possible solutions to one of the issues* that emerged in their survey.
I can carry out my responsibility as a citizen by determining an appropriate course of action for addressing a social issue. (F.8)	I can use sequence (first, second, third) to write a plan.	Students... • **Create a written plan of action** to *address the problem they identified.*

(continued)

Figure A.1 (*continued*)

RIGHTS AND OPPORTUNITIES UNIT

Learning Experiences *(abbreviated list)*—*(continued)*		
Learning Target	**Language Objective**	**Learning Activity**
I can reflect on my learning.	I can use past tense to describe what I felt before and present tense to describe how I feel now.	Students . . . • **Write a reflection** in which they share – *What they learned from their examination of the civil rights movement and their civic engagement experience.* – *How their ideas have changed/ remained the same when compared with their original thinking about the essential question "Do we all have the same rights and opportunities?"* – *How their learning may affect actions they take in their communities in the future.*

This unit is intentionally designed to incorporate all elements of a curriculum that matters. Each element can be identified by changing the lens through which the unit is viewed.

Practices: The practices that students use throughout the unit are clearly identified with the standards. These practices are used to write guiding questions for the unit: *What are the responsibilities of citizens of the United States? When is it necessary to take social action?* Students apply the practices in a culminating authentic task: taking action to address an inequity they see in their school.

Learning targets and the learning activities are strongly aligned to the practices. Students use practices that are applicable across disciplines, including analyzing sources from different perspectives, determining biases, and determining the evidence authors use to support their claims.

Deep Thinking: The essential question and big idea provide context for deep thinking. The curriculum-embedded performance assessment is a multistep, complex task that taps different ways of thinking that have been identified in the standards for the unit. This includes using the cognitive processes of evaluating and creating, while working with conceptual and metacognitive knowledge (as described in Bloom's taxonomy) for a real-world, unpredictable situation. Students use the creative process to generate and select an idea to carry out.

There are learning targets and activities that focus on specific cognitive processes. These include analyzing texts to determine authors' claims and the evidence used to support their claims, recognizing bias in texts, and evaluating situations based on a set of criteria.

Social and Emotional Learning: The unit is built on the competency of social awareness, as it brings student attention to the experience of others. A social and emotional competency is identified with the standards to communicate its importance as an outcome for the unit. The social and emotional competency is also addressed through a guiding question as a reminder of its role in the unit: *How can our ability to empathize lead to social action?*

Learning targets and activities focus on social and emotional skills. These include developing relationship skills by creating and using norms for participating in discussions, using self-management skills to carry out a plan of action, and developing social awareness by examining the role of bias in perspective.

Civic Engagement and Discourse: The practice selected for the unit explicitly focuses on civic engagement. Students take civic action through the performance assessment. Students first examine the principles of democracy and citizenship in the United States as the basis for the work they will do through the curriculum-embedded performance assessment. They read about the civil rights movement and the role of different leaders, individuals, and groups. Students conduct research to define educational equity and explore key court cases and policies that have improved equitable access in education for all students in the United States. Students then engage in their own inquiry of how educational equity is addressed in their own school and if there are any places for improvement. These actions replicate the process of active citizenship in the United States.

Students are given strategies for examining sources of the past, including using the acronym SOAP and asking the questions *What do I notice? What do I see that makes me say that? What more can I find out?* Both of these media literacy skills can be applied to issues of today, preparing students to be better consumers of the media they use to formulate their opinions.

Students have opportunities to engage in discourse and are prepared to do so by creating and testing their own norms for discussion. Students discuss questions that are open-ended (such as *When is it necessary to take social action?*) and generate many different opinions. Students are provided with protocols to help them successfully navigate these experiences and prepare for discussions outside school.

Students reflect on their civic engagement at the end of the unit by answering the questions *How have your ideas changed/remained the same when compared with your original thinking about rights and opportunities? How might your learning affect actions you take in your community in the future?*

Equity: Students select an issue under the umbrella of educational equity after an extensive investigation of what the term means. Their examination is not limited to a specific time period or group of people, even though the civil rights movement is explicitly examined to deepen understanding. Students determine the audience for their work and the best way to reach that audience, given the focus of their work.

Learning activities illustrate the importance of telling different stories. Students examine different beliefs and approaches to the civil rights movement, including those of people who opposed it. They are asked to probe deeper into accepted and traditional versions of stories that have been told, such as the story of Rosa Parks. Students learn strategies for examining perspectives and bias that they can apply when evaluating single stories they encounter when examining other historical and current events.

The performance assessment is a model for students of what it means to advocate for a social cause. Through this experience, students develop the understanding that they have control over change. Interaction within the school and local community connects students with people whom they otherwise may not meet and develops social capital for future relationships. The performance assessment helps students see how their involvement can have an impact on policies that directly affect their lives, creating an opening for civic equity in the future.

Standards and valued outcomes are made accessible to students through guiding questions, learning targets and language objectives, and strongly aligned learning activities. Students engage in feedback, providing an additional way to access the standards for the unit. This is most evident through the formative assessment/feedback cycle. All learning activities embed a formative assessment opportunity that teachers can use to monitor student understanding and adjust instruction. Students are provided a pathway through the curriculum-embedded performance assessments, with learning activities that focus on content, process, and metacognition, using tools and reflective activities that provide support but build autonomy.

Students engage in high-impact, active-learning strategies, including opportunities to work cooperatively, participate in discussions, and use cognitive routines. Group work includes writing summaries, writing and conducting the survey, and implementing an action plan to address inequity. Discourse is both formal and informal and involves the use of established norms, protocols, and reflection on the experience.

Throughout the unit, students used cognitive routines such as the acronym SOAP and self-questioning strategies to develop as independent learners. Students routinely set and monitor goals and engage in self- and peer feedback, to become assessment-capable learners. At the end of the unit, engaged in metacognition, they reflect on how they changed as a result of their experience.

Appendix B:
Design Checklist

This checklist organizes the five elements of a curriculum that matters using the attributes of quality curriculum: standards alignment and placement, organizing center, diversified assessment system, curriculum-embedded performance assessment, and learning activities (Lalor, 2017).

Alignment to Standards, Standards Placement, and Emphasis

☐ Valued outcomes of learning are explicitly identified, including standards, practices, and social and emotional competencies.

☐ Only standards that are taught and assessed are identified in the unit of study. All standards are taught and assessed over the year; no standards are eliminated from the curriculum because of concerns about students' "ability."

☐ Standards and other valued outcomes have been examined to ensure they require different levels of thinking.

☐ Standards are made accessible to students through learning targets and language objectives, rubrics and checklists, and related feedback opportunities.

Organizing Center (Unit Focus, Essential and Guiding Questions, Big Idea)

☐ Organizing centers focus on important concepts related to the social and emotional competencies, including the examination of identity, culture, and relationships.

☐ The organizing center communicates the most important learning for a unit of study and sets the context for deep thinking.

☐ The essential question is supported by guiding questions. Guiding questions demonstrate how the unit incorporates the different elements of a curriculum that matters.

Assessment Types and Moments

☐ Students reflect on the essential question throughout the unit; the teacher uses the reflections to monitor student understanding of the big idea.

☐ Classroom diagnostic assessments provide information about what students know and can do. They identify student assets and the starting point for instruction.

☐ Formative assessment opportunities are linked to the curriculum-embedded performance assessment and provide opportunities for feedback and revision supporting all students' attainment of high expectations.

☐ Formative assessment opportunities are embedded in daily lessons and provide teachers with information to adjust instruction and differentiate tools and strategies so all students can successfully engage in the learning experience.

☐ Formative assessments provide students with information about their strengths, needs, and next steps. Students are made aware of their assets and know how to use them to learn.

☐ A variety of different types of assessments are used as diagnostic and formative assessment to monitor student learning, adjust instruction, and provide feedback.

Curriculum-Embedded Performance Assessments

☐ The curriculum-embedded performance assessment measures the most important learning as articulated through the organizing center and strongly aligns to standards, practices, and other valued outcomes.

☐ The curriculum-embedded performance assessment engages students in deep thought by tapping different levels of cognition as students progress through multistep, complex tasks for authentic purposes and audiences. It may include opportunities for students to apply design thinking or creative thinking as approaches for addressing these tasks.

☐ Students use SEL skills while working through the curriculum-embedded performance assessment. These include self-management skills to complete multistep tasks, relationship skills to work with others, and self-reflection skills to set and monitor goals.

☐ Students engage in their community in authentic and meaningful ways, using place-based learning, service learning, or similar approaches to curriculum-embedded performance assessments. These experiences build human and social capital and encourage students to work to develop civic equity in their community.

☐ Curriculum-embedded performance assessments develop students' critical consciousness and provide students opportunities to respond to injustices they identify in the world around them.

☐ Community-based and curriculum-embedded performance assessments are grounded in the principles of democracy and citizenship of the United States.

☐ Curriculum-embedded performance assessments embrace the cultural and lived experiences of students by providing students with the opportunity to make decisions about what they will learn, how they will learn, and how they will share their learning.

☐ Curriculum-embedded performance assessments allow for the natural integration of content across disciplines.

Learning Experiences

☐ Learning targets and success criteria are used to articulate what students will learn and the process for learning.

☐ Language objectives complement learning targets and provide information about language structure, function, and vocabulary.

☐ Learning experiences provide a pathway for working through the curriculum-embedded performance assessments.

☐ Practices are leveraged across disciplines as strategies for learning.

☐ Students are taught specific skills to address different types of thinking.

☐ Students engage in steps of the design process or creative process, where suitable, as part of their learning experiences.

☐ Learning experiences embed social and emotional learning such as examining models of SEL in action, using protocols and other strategies for understanding different perspectives and developing empathy, and providing structures to develop relationships.

☐ Students routinely set and monitor goals and engage in self- and peer feedback, to become assessment-capable learners.

☐ Students develop metacognitive skills by reflecting on all aspects of their learning.

☐ Students are taught about growth mindset and habits of mind. They use self-questioning tools and prompts to develop their own favorable beliefs about their learning and navigate learning when it becomes difficult.

☐ Students learn how to select strategies, and adjust them when necessary, to become independent, self-regulated learners.

☐ Students use high-impact, active-learning strategies including opportunities to work cooperatively, participate in discussions, or use cognitive routines.

☐ Students routinely engage in discourse that challenges their thinking and helps them to understand experiences, beliefs, opinions, and perspectives other than their own.

☐ Students' work is grounded in research. They use media literacy skills that help them to discern the credibility of the resources they use.

☐ Text and other resources represent a wide range of cultures and identities, providing both windows and mirrors into different cultures and experiences and disrupting single-story representations of people and events.

☐ Technology resources are available to all students and are used to enhance the learning experiences.

References

Adichie, C. N. (2009, October 7). The danger of a single story [TED Talk]. TED Global 2009. Retrieved from https://www.ted.com/talks/chimamanda_ngozi_adichie_the_danger_of_a_single_story/transcript

Anderson, L. W., & Krathwohl, D. R. (Eds.). (2001). *A taxonomy for learning, teaching, and assessing: A revision of Bloom's taxonomy of educational objectives.* New York: Longman.

Baker, S., Lesaux, N., Jayanthi, M., Dimino, J., Proctor, C. P., Morris, J., Gersten, R., Haymond, K., Kieffer, M. J., Linan-Thompson, S., & Newman-Gonchar, R. (2014). *Teaching academic content and literacy to English learners in elementary and middle school* (NCEE 2014-4012). Washington, DC: National Center for Education Evaluation and Regional Assistance (NCEE), Institute of Education Sciences, and U.S. Department of Education. Retrieved from the NCEE website: http://ies.ed.gov/ncee/wwc/publications_reviews.aspx

Battelle for Kids. (2018). Portrait of a graduate. Retrieved from https://portraitofagraduate.org/

Beck, I. L., McKeown, M. G., & Kucan, L. (2013). *Bringing words to life: Robust vocabulary instruction* (2nd ed.). New York: Guilford Press.

Boaler, J. (n.d.). *Number talks.* Youcubed. Retrieved from https://www.youcubed.org/resources/stanford-onlines-learn-math-teachers-parents-number-talks/

Bryan-Gooden, J., Hester, M. & Peoples, L. Q. (2019). *Culturally responsive curriculum scorecard.* New York: Metropolitan Center for Research on Equity and the Transformation of Schools, New York University.

Chideya, F. (Host). (2007, September 24). *Walking to class, into the history books* (audio podcast). Retrieved from *NPR* at https://www.npr.org/transcripts/14656178

Collaborative for Academic, Social, and Emotional Learning (CASEL). (2020). Framework for systematic social and emotional learning. Retrieved from https://casel.org/what-is-sel/

College Board. (2012). *The College Board history framework.* Available: https://www.collegeboard.org/pdf/history-framework-academic-advisory-committee.pdf

Collins, C. (2017, November). *Learning the landscape of digital literacy: An introduction for educators.* Montgomery, AL. Teaching Tolerance: A Project of the Southern Poverty Law Center. Retrieved from https://www.tolerance.org/sites/default/files/2017-11/Learning-the-Landscape-of-Digital-Literacy-Nov2017.pdf

Common Core State Standards (CCSS). (2019). *Standards for mathematical practice*. Available: http://www.corestandards.org/Math/Practice/

Costa, A. L., & Kallick, B. (2000). *Discovering & exploring habits of mind*. Alexandria, VA: ASCD.

Costa, A. L., & Kallick, B. (2008). *Learning and leading with habits of mind*. Alexandria, VA: ASCD.

Cunningham, D. (2020, April 23). Three moves to elevate student discussion. *ASCD Express, 15*(16). Retrieved from http://www.ascd.org/ascd-express/vol15/num16/three-moves-to-elevate-student-discussion.aspx

d.school. (n.d.). *An introduction to design thinking: Process guide*. Stanford, CA: Hasso-Plattner Institute. Retrieved from https://s3-eu-west-1.amazonaws.com/ih-materials/uploads/Introduction-to-design-thinking.pdf

Dam, R. F., & Siang, T. Y. (2020). *5 stages in the design thinking process*. Interaction Design Foundation. Retrieved from https://www.interaction-design.org/literature/article/5-stages-in-the-design-thinking-process

de Bono, E. (n.d.). *Six thinking hats*. The de Bono Group. Retrieved from https://www.debonogroup.com/services/core-programs/six-thinking-hats/

Drapeau, P. (2014). *Sparking student creativity: Practical ways to promote innovative thinking and problem solving*. Alexandria, VA: ASCD

Du Bois, W. E. B. (1920). *Darkwater: Voices from within the veil*. New York: Harcourt, Brace.

Dunbar-Ortiz, R. (2014). *An Indigenous peoples' history of the United States*. Boston: Beacon Press.

Dweck, C. S. (2006) *Mindset: The new psychology of success: How we can learn to fulfill our potential*. New York: Ballantine Books.

Ehrlich, T. (Ed.). (2000). *Civic responsibility and higher education*. Westport, CT: Oryx Press.

English Learners Success Forum (ELSF). (n.d.). *ELA best practices, must haves, and pitfalls*. Retrieved from https://www.elsuccessforum.org/resources/ela-best-practices-must-haves-and-pitfalls

Feige, D. (2010). Mapping slippery transformative (service learning) roads. In R. Verma (Ed.), *Be the change: Teacher, activist, global citizen* (Ch. 5). New York: Peter Lang.

Finley, T. (2014, February 19). *Common Core in action: 10 visual literacy strategies*. Edutopia. Retrieved from http://www.edutopia.org/blog/ccia-10-visual-literacy-strategies-todd-finley

Frey, N., Hattie, J., & Fisher, D. (2018). *Developing assessment-capable visible learners, grades K–12: Maximizing skill, will, and thrill*. Thousand Oaks, CA: Corwin.

Glossary of Education Reform. (2013). Growth mindset. Available: https://www.edglossary.org/growth-mindset/

Gould, J. (Ed.). (2011). *Guardian of democracy: The civic mission of schools*. Philadelphia: Leonore Annenberg Institute for Civics at the University of Pennsylvania. Retrieved from https://media.carnegie.org/filer_public/ab/dd/abdda62e-6e84-47a4-a043-348d2f2085ae/ccny_grantee_2011_guardian.pdf

Halvorsen, A.-L., & Duke, N. K. (2017, June 20). Project-based learning: Raising student achievement for all learners. *Edutopia*. Retrieved from https://www.edutopia.org/video/project-based-learning-raising-student-achievement-all-learners

Hammond, Z. (2015). *Culturally responsive teaching and the brain: Promoting authentic engagement and rigor among culturally and linguistically diverse students*. Thousand Oaks, CA: Corwin.

Hattie, J. (2009). *Visible learning*. New York: Routledge.

Hattie, J. (2012). *Visible learning for teachers: Maximizing impact on learning*. New York: Routledge.

Hattie, J. (2017). Distinguishing surface and deep learning (Video). UQx: LEARNx Deep Learning Through Transformative Pedagogy. University of Queensland, Australia (an Open edX MOOC). Module 1: Surface and Deep Learning. Retrieved from https://granite.pressbooks.pub/teachingdiverselearners/chapter/surface-and-deep-learning-2/

Henkes, K. (1990). *Julius, the baby of the world.* New York: HarperCollins.

Henkes, K. (1996). *Lilly's purple plastic purse.* New York: HarperCollins.

Hess, D. (2009). *Controversy in the classroom: The democratic power of discussion.* New York: Routledge.

Himmel, J. (2012). Language objectives: The key to effective content area instruction for English learners. *Colorín Colorado.* Retrieved from https://www.colorincolorado.org/article/language-objectives-key-effective-content-area-instruction-english-learners

Hobbs, R. (2020, March 28). Online learning and media literacy [Blog post]. Media Education Lab. Retrieved from https://mediaedlab.com/2020/03/28/online-learning-media-literacy/

Hyerle, D. (2008). *Visual tools for transforming information into knowledge* (2nd ed.). Thousand Oaks, CA: Corwin.

Jackson, Y. (2016, February). Transformational pedagogy: Cashing the promissory note of equity for marginalized students and all students. In *Equity-centered capacity building: Essential approaches for excellence and sustainable school system transformation* (pp. 78–92). Equity-Centered Capacity-Building Network (ECCBN).

Kaye, C. B. (2004). *The complete guide to service learning: Proven, practical ways to engage students in civic responsibility, academic curriculum, and social action.* Minneapolis, MN: Free Spirit Publishing.

Ladson-Billings, G. (2014, April). Culturally relevant pedagogy 2.0: a.k.a. the remix. *Harvard Educational Review, 84*(1), 74–84. Retrieved from https://doi.org/10.17763/haer.84.1.p2rj131485484751

Lalor, A. D. (2012). Keeping the destination in mind. *Educational Leadership, 70*(1), 75–78.

Lalor, A. D. (2017). *Ensuring high-quality curriculum: How to design, revise, or adopt curriculum aligned to student success.* Alexandria, VA: ASCD.

Lander, J. (December 2019/January 2020). Seeing their strengths. *Educational Leadership, 77*(4), 24–28.

Margolick, D. (2012). *Elizabeth and Hazel: Two women of Little Rock.* New Haven, CT: Yale University Press.

McTighe, J., & Silver, H. F. (2020). *Teaching for deeper learning: Tools for engaging students in meaning making.* Alexandria, VA: ASCD.

Milne, A. A. (1996). *The complete works of Winnie the Pooh.* New York: Dutton Children's Books.

Milner, H. R. (2017, November). Reimagining the null curriculum. *Educational Leadership, 75*(3), 88–89.

National Association for Media Literacy Education (NAMLE). (n.d.) Who is NAMLE? Retrieved from https://medialiteracyweek.us/about/who-is-namle/

National Coalition for Core Arts Standards (NCCAS). (2014). *National Core Arts Standards.* Retrieved from: https://www.nationalartsstandards.org/

National Research Council. (2013). *Next Generation Science Standards: For states, by states.* Washington, DC: National Academies Press. Available: https://doi.org/10.17226/18290

National Youth Leadership Council (NYLC). (n.d.) What is service-learning? Retrieved from https://www.nylc.org/page/WhatisService-Learning

New York State Education Department (NYSED). (2017a). *New York State next generation English language arts learning standards.* Retrieved from http://www.nysed

.gov/common/nysed/files/programs/curriculum-instruction/nys-next-generation-ela-standards.pdf

New York State Education Department (NYSED). (2017b). *New York State K–8 social studies framework*. Retrieved from https://www.engageny.org/resource/new-york-state-k-12-social-studies-framework

New York State Education Department (NYSED). (2017c). *New York State 9–12 social studies framework*. Retrieved from https://www.engageny.org/resource/new-york-state-k-12-social-studies-framework

New York State Education Department (NYSED). (2018, August). *New York State social emotional learning benchmarks*. Retrieved from http://www.p12.nysed.gov/sss/sel-benchmarks.html

New York Times. (n.d.). What's going on in this picture? Learning Network. Retrieved from https://www.nytimes.com/column/learning-whats-going-on-in-this-picture

Polacco, P. (1990). *Thunder cake*. New York: Philomel Books.

Project Zero. (2019). Word-phrase-sentence [thinking routine]. Harvard Graduate School of Education. Available: http://pz.harvard.edu/resources/sentence-phrase-word

Resnick, L. B., & Hall, M. W. (2003). *Principles of learning: Study tools for educators*. Pittsburgh, PA: University of Pittsburgh.

Rogers, J. (2019, February 26). *An equitable approach to strengthening civic education*. New York: Center for Educational Equity at Teachers College, Columbia University.

Ronan, B. (2011). The civic spectrum: How students become engaged. Kettering Foundation. Retrieved from https://files.eric.ed.gov/fulltext/ED539344.pdf

Saavedra, E., & Nolan. E. (2018, November). Toward transformative social and emotional learning: Using an equity lens. *Summary Brief for Special Issues Brief on Equity*. Retrieved from https://measuringsel.casel.org/wp-content/uploads/2018/11/Framework_EquitySummary-.pdf

School Reform Initiative (SRI). (n.d.). Four A's text protocol. Adapted from Judith Gray, Seattle, WA, 2005. Retrieved from https://www.schoolreforminitiative.org/download/four-as-text-protocol/

Shannon, D. (1998). *No, David!* New York: Blue Sky Press.

Share, J., Jolls, T., & Thoman, E. (2005). *Five key questions that can change the world: Lesson plans for media literacy*. Malibu, CA: Center for Media Literacy. Retrieved from http://www.medialit.org/sites/default/files/5KQ%20ClassroomGuide_1.pdf

Smith, D., Frey, N., Pumpian, I., & Fisher, D. (2017*). Building equity: Policies and practices to empower all learners*. Alexandria, VA: ASCD.

Stockman, A. (2020). *Creating inclusive writing environments in the K–12 classroom: Reluctance, resistance, and strategies that make a difference*. New York: Routledge.

Stuve-Bodeen, S. (2000). *Elizabeti's doll*. New York: Lee & Lows Books.

Style, E. (1996, Fall). Curriculum as window and mirror. *Social Science Record, 33*(2), 21–28. Available: https://nationalseedproject.org/images/documents/Curriculum_As_Window_and_Mirror.pdf

Tripodo, A., & Pondscio, R. (2017, November). Seizing the civic education moment. *Educational Leadership, 75*(3), 20–25.

Tschida, C. M., Ryan. C. L., & Ticknor, A. S. (2014, Spring). Building on windows and mirrors: Encouraging the disruption of "single stories" through children's literature. *Journal of Children's Literature, 40*(1), 28–39.

Vilen, A., & Berger, R. (2020, April). Courageous conversations for equity and agency. *Educational Leadership, 77*(7), 39–44.

Wade, R. (2009, May). A pebble in a pond. *Educational Leadership, 66*(8), 50–53.

Weiner, C. (n.d.). Want to facilitate role playing in your class? Harvard ABLConnect. Retrieved from https://ablconnect.harvard.edu/want-facilitate-role-playing-your-class

Weissberg, R. P., Durlack, J. A., Domitrovich, C. E., & Gullotta, T. P. (Eds.). (2015). Social and emotional learning: Past, present, and future. In J. A. Durlak, C. E. Domitrovich, R. P. Weissberg, & T. P. Gullotta (Eds.), *Handbook of social and emotional learning: Research and practice* (pp. 3–19). New York: Guilford Press.

Wiggins, G., & McTighe, J. (2005). *Understanding by Design* (2nd expanded ed.). Alexandria, VA: ASCD.

Willems, M. (2005). *The pigeon has feelings, too*. New York: Disney-Hyperion.

Winthrop, R., & Heubeck, M. (2019). The bucket list for involved citizens: 76 things you can do to boost civic engagement. Brookings Institution. Available: https://www.brookings.edu/blog/education-plus-development/2019/11/12/the-bucket-list-for-involved-citizens-76-things-you-can-do-to-boost-civic-engagement/

Wolpert-Gawron, H. (2016, November 7). What the heck is service learning? *Edutopia*. Available: https://www.edutopia.org/blog/what-heck-service-learning-heather-wolpert-gawron

Yale University Center for Emotional Intelligence. (n.d.). Mood meter. Retrieved from https://www.rulerapproach.org/

Zimmerman, B. J. (2000). Self-efficacy: An essential motive to learn. *Contemporary Educational Psychology, 25*(1), 82–91. Retrieved from https://www.sciencedirect.com/science/article/pii/S0361476X99910160

Index

The letter *f* following a page locator denotes a figure.

About the Author

**Angela Di Michele Lalor** is a national educational consultant who has facilitated schoolwide professional development initiatives for more than 20 years. Her primary focus has been helping districts develop curriculum, assessment, and instruction practices that reflect the vision and mission of their schools. A recognized expert in curriculum design, Angela believes that curriculum is an underused tool that, when aligned to valued outcomes, can greatly improve student experiences in the classroom.

She is also the author of *Ensuring High-Quality Curriculum: How to Design, Revise, or Adopt Curriculum Aligned to Student Success*, which provides a comprehensive guide for educators looking to create, revise, or evaluate curriculum. Angela presents nationally for ASCD.

Additional information about Angela and her work is available at adlalorconsulting.com. She can be reached at angela@adlalor consulting.com and found on LinkedIn (www.linkedin.com/in/angela-di-michele-lalor-2319677b/) and Twitter (@ADiLalor).

Related ASCD Resources

At the time of publication, the following resources were available (ASCD stock numbers in parentheses).

Becoming a Globally Competent Teacher by Ariel Tichnor-Wagner, Hillary Parkhouse, Jocelyn Glazier, and J. Montana Cain (#119012)

Bold Moves for Schools: How We Create Remarkable Learning Environments by Heidi Hayes Jacobs and Marie Hubley Alcock (#115013)

Designing Authentic Performance Tasks and Projects: Tools for Meaningful Learning and Assessment by Jay McTighe, Kristina J. Doubet, and Eric M. Carbaugh (#119021)

Ensuring High-Quality Curriculum: How to Design, Revise, or Adopt Curriculum Aligned to Student Success by Angela Di Michele Lalor (#116006)

The Equity & Social Justice Education 50: Critical Questions for Improving Opportunities and Outcomes for Black Students by Baruti K. Kafele (#121060)

Essential Questions: Opening Doors to Student Understanding by Jay McTighe and Grant Wiggins (#109004)

The i5 Approach: Lesson Planning That Teaches Thinking and Fosters Innovation by Jane E. Pollock with Susan Hensley (#117030)

Improve Every Lesson Plan with SEL by Jeffrey Benson (#121057)

Taking Social-Emotional Learning Schoolwide: The Formative Five Success Skills for Students and Staff by Thomas R. Hoerr (#120014)

Teaching for Deeper Learning: Tools to Engage Students in Meaning Making by Jay McTighe and Harvey F. Silver (#120022)

Using Understanding by Design in the Culturally and Linguistically Diverse Classroom by Amy J. Heineke and Jay McTighe (#118084)

For up-to-date information about ASCD resources, go to **www.ascd.org.** You can search the complete archives of *Educational Leadership* at **www.ascd.org/el.**

ASCD myTeachSource®
Download resources from a professional learning platform with hundreds of research-based best practices and tools for your classroom at http://myteachsource.ascd.org/

For more information, send an email to member@ascd.org; call 1-800-933-2723 or 703-578-9600; send a fax to 703-575-5400; or write to Information Services, ASCD, 1703 N. Beauregard St., Alexandria, VA 22311-1714 USA.

THE WHOLE CHILD

The ASCD Whole Child approach is an effort to transition from a focus on narrowly defined academic achievement to one that promotes the long-term development and success of all children. Through this approach, ASCD supports educators, families, community members, and policymakers as they move from a vision about educating the whole child to sustainable, collaborative actions.

Making Curriculum Matter relates to the **safe, engaged,** and **challenged** tenets. *For more about the ASCD Whole Child approach, visit* **www.ascd. org/wholechild.**

WHOLE CHILD
TENETS

1 HEALTHY
Each student enters school healthy and learns about and practices a healthy lifestyle.

2 SAFE
Each student learns in an environment that is physically and emotionally safe for students and adults.

3 ENGAGED
Each student is actively engaged in learning and is connected to the school and broader community.

4 SUPPORTED
Each student has access to personalized learning and is supported by qualified, caring adults.

5 CHALLENGED
Each student is challenged academically and prepared for success in college or further study and for employment and participation in a global environment.